An Introduction to Phonics

Phonemes

and

Graphemes

WORD BANKS

Barrina J Mills

Emerald Torrus Publishers

Published by **Emerald Torrus Publishers**

Paperback - ISBN 9781068656507

info@emeraldtorrus.com

Note from the Author

Thank you for purchasing this phonics reference book. I hope it simplifies the teaching and learning of phonics for you.

As a qualified NNEB Nursery Nurse and an experienced Higher Level Teaching Assistant, I spent 25 years in a London primary school, supporting students in Early Years, Key Stage 1 and Key Stage 2, across all areas of their learning and development.

Over time, I specialized in teaching phonics to Early Years and Key Stage 1, creating fun booster classes for those who had difficulty with reading and spelling. My own childhood struggles had fuelled my passion for teaching children these critical life skills.

I also developed a simple phonics training workshop for trainee teachers and support staff, which also served as a refresher for those who hadn't taught phonics in a while.

I take great pride in my continuous efforts to further my education and share my skills and knowledge. It brings me joy to know that, through this reference book, I will continue to provide support and guidance for those who need a little extra help in teaching phonics.

The idea to create this reference book came to me in 2016, after struggling to find suitable word banks, for my phonics booster classes, that were easy to access. Putting it all together ended up taking far longer than I'd expected - a total of eight years. I would work on it for a few weeks or a month at a time, then set it aside for several months or even a year before returning to it.

Each time I thought the book was complete, I would find more content to include and ways to improve it. Editing, formatting, and proofreading presented its challenges and at times I had felt overwhelmed and disheartened, even doubting my abilities, but I remained committed to finishing what I had started.

This year, I was more determined than ever to finish my book and share it with you. Through sheer determination and perseverance, what started as sheets of paper in a purple folder has finally transformed into a real book.

As I write this in 2024, I feel immensely proud of my achievement.

Acknowledgements

A sincere thank you goes out to my family, friends, and all who offered support, used my resources in their classrooms and gave positive feedback and encouragement, throughout the process of creating this reference book. I choose not to mention specific names to avoid overlooking anyone, but each of you knows your valuable contributions. I am extremely grateful!! Thank you.

Phonics is a method of teaching the relationship between **phonemes** (sounds) and **graphemes** (written symbols/letters), in order to read.

Contents

Page

Colour coding is used throughout this book for easy referencing.

Letter/s placed between forward slashes (/a/) refers to the phoneme (sound).
Letter/s written in green refers to the grapheme (letter name/s).

The terms "phoneme/s" and "sound/s" are used interchangeably, throughout this reference book.

The initial grapheme-phoneme correspondence (GPC) highlighted in this book is represented by a circle (●).
Typically, this is introduced in Reception class or for those new to British English. Following this, squares (■) are taught in Year 1, then diamonds (◆) in Year 2 and above.

Lists of alternative graphemes are organized alphabetically within their color-coded groups and are not in a specific order of learning. For instance, for the /igh/ phoneme (pg47), the grapheme 'igh' is categorized under the circle (●) symbol, but some Systematic Synthetic Phonics (SSP) programmes may introduce the 'ie' spelling first, along with other alternative graphemes at different stages or in a specific order.

● Reception Class/New to English ■ Year 1 ◆ Year 2 and above

An Introduction to Phonics **Phonemes to Graphemes Word Bank** Copyright ©2024 Barrina J Mills

Vowel Phonemes	International Phonetic Alphabet	Graphemes						page
/a/	æ	● apple	◆ meringue					15
/ai/	eɪ	● rain	■ table	■ cake	■ day	◆ great	■ eight	17
		◆ reggae	◆ straight	◆ vein	◆ bouquet	◆ grey		
/air/	eə	● chair	■ parent	■ dairy	■ scare	■ pear	■ where	19
		◆ aerial	◆ billionaire	◆ scarce	◆ their	◆ heiress	◆ heirloom	
/ar/	ɑː	● artist	■ father	◆ blah	◆ half	◆ laugh	◆ heart	21
/e/	e	● egg	■ said	■ bread	◆ any	◆ leisure	◆ leopard	31
		◆ friend	◆ bury					
/ear/	ɪə	● year	■ cheer	◆ era	◆ idea	◆ eerie	◆ madeira	33
		◆ weird	◆ adhere	◆ cashier				
/ee/	iː	● green	■ me	■ complete	■ eat	■ key [1]	■ monkey [2]	35
		■ fifty	◆ algae	◆ quay	◆ seizure	◆ people	◆ machine	
		◆ piece	◆ coeliac					
/er/	ɜː	● person	■ were	■ girl	■ work	■ nurse	◆ early	37
		◆ journal						
/i/	ɪ	● milk	■ planted	◆ orange	◆ fountain	◆ below	◆ sieve	45
		◆ women	◆ busy	◆ build	◆ crystal			
/igh/	aɪ	● light	■ eyebrow	■ bike	■ pie	■ my	◆ eider	47
		◆ height	◆ blind	◆ fire	◆ island	◆ buy	◆ bye	
/o/	ɒ	● clock	■ what	◆ yacht	◆ because	◆ cough		59
/oa/	əʊ	● boat	■ over	■ phone	■ blow	■ mauve	◆ bureau	61
		◆ sew	◆ oboe	◆ brooch	◆ bouquet	◆ dough		
/oi/	ɔɪ	● voice	■ royal					63
long /OO/	uː	● school	■ screw	■ do	■ flute	■ blue	■ two	65
		◆ shoe	◆ soup	◆ through	◆ truth	◆ fruit		
short /OO/	ʊ	● cook	■ push	◆ wolf	◆ should			67
/or/	ɔː	● fork	■ ball	■ walk	■ autumn	■ caught	■ crawl	69
		■ story	■ door	◆ swarm	◆ dinosaur	◆ broad	◆ boards	
		◆ shore	◆ bought	◆ four				
/ou/	aʊ	● cloud	■ cow	◆ hour	◆ flour	◆ plough		71
/u/	ʌ	● fun	■ son	■ blood	◆ does	◆ touch		89
/ue/	juː	● value	■ new	■ unicorn	■ perfume	◆ beauty	◆ feud	91
		◆ view	◆ vacuum	◆ youth				
schwa /uh/	ə	● paper	■ pizza	■ open [1]	■ apple [2]	■ family	■ dozen	93
		■ joyful [1]	◆ sugar	◆ actor	◆ famous	◆ borough	◆ colour	
		◆ focus [2]	◆ our	◆ nature [1]	◆ mature [2]	◆ secure [3]		

Note: While it is not necessary to learn the International Phonetic Alphabet, understanding its use can be helpful.

● Reception Class/New to English   ■ Year 1   ◆ Year 2 and above

An Introduction to Phonics **Phonemes to Graphemes Word Bank** Copyright ©2024 Barrina J Mills

Consonant Phonemes	International Phonetic Alphabet	Graphemes						page
/b/	b	● **b**ird	● ri**bb**on					23
/c/ /k/	k	● **c**at	● chi**ck**	■ **k**iss	◆ o**cc**ur	◆ s**ch**ool	◆ a**ch**e	25
		◆ ra**cqu**et	◆ tre**kk**ed	◆ bou**qu**et	◆ uni**qu**e			
/ch/	tʃ	● **ch**at	◆ **c**ello	◆ for**t**une	◆ ba**tch**			27
/d/	d	● **d**ay	● mi**dd**le	■ play**ed**	■ love**d**			29
/f/	f	● **f**amily	● pu**ff**	■ **ph**onics	◆ cou**gh**			39
/g/	g	● **g**ood	● fo**gg**y	◆ **gh**erkin	◆ **gu**ess	◆ lea**gu**e	◆ e**x**act	41
/h/	h	● **h**appy	◆ **wh**ole					43
/j/	dʒ	● **j**oy	■ e**dge**	■ **g**erm	■ oran**ge**	◆ ostri**ch**	◆ e**d**ucate	49
		◆ a**dj**oin	◆ ve**gg**ie					
/l/	l	● **l**uck	● je**ll**y	■ sty**le** ₁	■ tab**le** ₂			51
/m/	m	● **m**agic	● yu**mm**y	■ **c**ome	◆ phle**gm**	◆ thu**mb**	◆ autu**mn**	53
/n/	n	● **n**eedle	● fu**nn**y	■ **kn**it	◆ **gn**ome	◆ **pn**eumatic		55
/ng/	ŋ	● so**ng**	◆ a**n**kle	◆ to**ngue**				57
/p/	p	● **p**arty	● ha**pp**y					73
/qu/	k + w	● **qu**ick	◆ ac**qu**it					75
/r/	r	● **r**ain	● so**rr**y	■ **wr**ong	◆ **rh**ino			77
/s/	s	● **s**ing	● dre**ss**	■ **c**ity	■ dan**ce**	■ hor**se**	■ li**s**ten	79
		◆ **ps**ycho	◆ **sc**ent	◆ **s**word	◆ wal**tz**			
/sh/	ʃ	● **sh**out	◆ o**ce**an	◆ **ch**ef	◆ qui**che**	◆ spe**ci**al	◆ **s**ugar	81
		◆ ten**si**on	◆ ti**ss**ue	◆ pa**ss**ion	◆ fi**c**tion			
/t/	t	● **t**iger	● bu**tt**on	■ jump**ed**	■ bas**te**	◆ dou**b**t	◆ recei**p**t	83
Voiced /th/	ð	● **th**is	■ brea**the**					85
Unvoiced /th/	θ	● au**th**or						87
/v/	v	● **v**est	■ o**f**	■ cur**ve**	◆ sa**vv**y			95
/w/	w	● **w**atch	■ **o**ne	■ **wh**ale	◆ pen**gu**in			97
/x/	k + s	● bo**x**	◆ e**x**cite	◆ delu**xe**				99
/y/	j	● **y**ellow						101
/z/	z	● **z**oom	● pu**zz**le	■ boy**s**	■ chee**se**	■ bree**ze**	■ busine**ss**	103
		◆ de**ss**ert	◆ an**x**iety ₁	◆ e**x**am ₂				
/zh/	ʒ	◆ **g**enre	◆ rou**ge**	◆ ca**s**ual	◆ vi**s**ion	◆ equa**ti**on	◆ sei**z**ure	105

PHONEME

A **phoneme** is the smallest unit of **sound** in speech.
Phonemes *(sounds)* are represented by different **graphemes** *(written symbols/letters)*.
There are **44 phonemes** in the English language.

Phonemes	Graphemes				
/ai/	acorn	grain	eight	great	stray
/ee/	me	swede	teach	bee	fields
/j/	spinach	bridge	germ	large	jazz
/or/	August	taught	crawl	short	snore
/s/	prince	sand	horse	dress	listen

GRAPHEME

A **grapheme** is a **letter** or group of **letters** that represent the **sounds** in speech.
Graphemes *(written symbols/letters)* can be represented by different **phonemes** *(sounds)*.
There are over **150 graphemes** in the English language.

Graphemes	Phonemes		
a	/ai/ table	/air/ parent	/or/ water
ea	/ai/ break	/e/ bread	/ee/ breathe
ear	/air/ swear	/ear/ beard	/er/ earth
o	/o/ clock	/oa/ over	/u/ son

DIGRAPH

A **digraph** is a group of **two letters** creating a single **phoneme**.

Digraphs can be a vowel or consonant phoneme

ai	ar	ee	ie	oo
mail	smart	sweet	tries	blood
or	**ue**	**ck**	**ph**	**se**
word	value	click	dolphin	horse

TRIGRAPH

A trigraph is a group of three letters creating a single phoneme.

Trigraphs can be a vowel or consonant phoneme

air	ear	igh
f**air**	y**ear**	br**igh**t
ore	dge	tch
sn**ore**	fri**dge**	ma**tch**

QUADGRAPH

A quadgraph is a group of four letters creating a single phoneme.

Quadgraphs are usually vowel phonemes

aigh	augh
str**aigh**t	d**augh**ter
eigh	ough
eighteen	th**ough**t

SPLIT VOWEL DIGRAPH

**A split vowel digraph is created when a long vowel digraph,
which sounds like the name of its first letter and ends with an 'E', is split by a consonant.**

/ai/ ae	/ee/ ee	/igh/ ie	/oa/ oe	/ue/ ue
'a' split 'e'	'e' split 'e'	'i' split 'e'	'o' split 'e'	'u' split 'e'
cake	athlete	drive	broke	amuse
blame	compete	inside	grove	cute
grape	delete	price	hope	excuse
same	scene	smile	nose	tube
shape	theme	time	throne	volume

DIPHTHONG

**A diphthong is a combination of two phonemes, which blends into each other
to produce a long vowel sound.**

di means *two*   **phthong** means *sound*

The following vowel digraphs & trigraphs are **diphthongs**.

/ou/, /oi/, /ai/, /oa/, /ear/, /air/, /igh/

If you place your hands on your cheeks and say each of the above sounds slowly,
you can feel how your mouth moves from one position to another.

Keep your hands on your cheeks and say the following sounds:

/sh/, /ch/, /f/, /a/, /mm/, /th/, /or/

Your mouth will stay in the same position. These are referred to as **pure sounds**.

SCHWA or shwa

Schwa (ə) is the most common vowel phoneme in the English language.
The schwa (pronounced sh - w - ar) is the /uh/ sound you hear in words
and can be represented by all of the vowels.

There are over 15 graphemes for this phoneme.

amaze	pillar	taken	farmer
April	today	doctor	nature

INTERNATIONAL PHONETIC ALPHABET – IPA

A standardised set of symbols representing the sounds of speech.

	Phonemes	IPA symbols
learn	/l/ - /er/ - /n/	l - ɜː - n
heart	/h/ - /ar/ - /t/	h - ɑː - t
phonics	/f/ - /o/ - /n/ - /i/ - /k/ - /s/	f - ɒ - n - ɪ - k - s
cycling	/s/ - /igh/ - /k/ - /l/ - /i/ - /ng/	s - aɪ - k - l - ɪ - ŋ
watch	/w/ - /o/ - /ch/	w - ɒ - tʃ
question	/k/ - /w/ - /e/ - /s/ - /ch/ - /uh/ - /n/	k - w - e - s - tʃ - ə - n

GRAPHEME - PHONEME CORRESPONDENCES - GPC

This is a list of the 44 grapheme/phoneme correspondences.

/a/	apple	/b/	bell	/c/	cake	/d/	dish	/e/	enjoy	/f/	flag
/g/	gift	/h/	hard	/i/	insect	/j/	jump	/k/	kiss	/l/	lemon
/m/	map	/n/	neck	/o/	off	/p/	pink	/qu/	quick	/r/	rain
/s/	sun	/t/	tax	/u/	up	/v/	vet	/w/	wind	/x/	fix
/y/	yes	/z/	zip	/ai/	tail	/air/	chair	/ar/	card	/ch/	chin
/ear/	dear	/ee/	feel	/er/	kerb	/igh/	tight	/ng/	sing	/oa/	soap
/oi/	foil	long /oo/	food	short /oo/	cook	/or/	born	/ou/	loud	/sh/	shut
unvoiced /th/	three	voiced /th/	they	/ue/	value	schwa /uh/	dinner	/zh/	vision		

Although /qu/ and /x/ are both taught as single phonemes, they are both made up of two sounds.
The /qu/ is usually made up of /k/ +/w/ as in 'quick', or the single phoneme /k/ as in 'bouquet'
The /x/ is made up of /k/ + /s/ as in 'extra' or made up of /g/ + /z/ as in 'example'. Therefore, /qu/ and /x/ are not true phonemes. They can still be found individually in the word bank (pg75 and pg99).
The /c/ and /k/ are the same phoneme and the graphemes 'c', 'k' and 'ck' are usually taught at the same time.
The schwa /uh/, often called the 'lazy vowel', is not always taught in schools.
The /zh/ is not usually taught until Year 3 or 4.
The /f/, /v/ and both the voiced and unvoiced /th/ are often mispronounced. Support students by making sure that the tongue, lips and teeth are placed correctly for each phoneme, especially when they first learn these sounds, as it can be harder to correct later.

SUPPORTING YOUR STUDENTS.

Make sure you are pronouncing each phoneme correctly, especially when your students are very young.
Practice: Say the word "jam" a few times and really pay attention to the first and last sounds. The 'J' has a short gentle sound, not a heavy *j-uh*. The 'M' is pronounced *mmm* not *m-uh*. Now take your time to read through the following examples, giving an extra focus to both the voiced and unvoiced consonants. Remember, /qu/ and /x/ are both made up of two phonemes (see pg10), so they are not listed in the examples below.

When teaching your students, make sure you are speaking clearly. Listen closely to how they repeat the phoneme back to you. Don't worry if they are unable to say the sound correctly, at first. Always confirm the phoneme once more, so that the final sound they hear is always correct.

Short Vowel	Unvoiced Consonant	Voiced Consonant
/a/ as in bat and sand	/ch/ as in chin and witch	/b/ as in bag and rubbish
/e/ as in ten and bread	/f/ as in fan and puff	/d/ as in dig and muddy
/i/ as in skin and event	/h/ as in help and who	/g/ as in get and bigger
/o/ as in frog and wash	/k/ as in sink and cot	/j/ as in jam and germ
/u/ as in jug and love	/p/ as in pet and slipper	/l/ as in lisp and smell
/oo/ as in shook and push	/s/ as in set and mess	/m/ as in moth and simmer
	/sh/ as in dish and chef	/n/ as in snap and tennis
	/t/ as in gift and bottle	/ng/ as in bring and pink
	/th/ as in thank and truth	/r/ as in rag and arrow
Long Vowel		/th/ as in them and breathe
		/v/ as in brave and give
/ar/ as in card and spa	**Long Vowel** (Diphthong)	/w/ as in water and when
/ee/ as in sleep and swede	/ai/ as in rain and take	/y/ as in yell and yuck
/er/ as in term and bird	/air/ as in chair and square	/z/ as in maze and jazz
/oo/ as in food and grew	/ear/ as in year and cheer	/zh/ as in leisure and vision
/or/ as in fork and ball	/igh/ as in sigh and smile	**Schwa**
/ue/ as in value and mute	/oa/ as in soap and rose	
	/oi/ as in soil and enjoy	/uh/ as in over and pizza
	/ou/ as in mouse and brown	

The first grapheme-phoneme correspondence (GPC) to be introduced, in this book, is coded with a circle (●).

● Reception Class/New to English	■ Year 1	◆ Year 2 and above	
Alternative graphemes for the phoneme /ee/			
● ee	■ e	■ e-e	■ ea
feet green sleep	be he we	athlete complete delete	beach cream teach
■ ey	■ y	◆ ae	◆ ei
monkey	fifty	algae larvae	ceiling deceive
◆ eo	◆ i	◆ ie	◆ oe
people	machine police	believe chief	coeliac phoenix

When introducing a phoneme, select 6 to 10 words from the chosen grapheme word bank that are relevant to the students' age and understanding. Write each word on a visual board, pronouncing each one slowly and highlighting the focus phoneme. Ask the students to repeat each word after you. Can they hear and identify where the focus phoneme is in the word? It may be the first sound that they hear, the last sound, or it could be (somewhere) in the middle of the word. Older students can pronounce each phoneme and be more specific with their answers.

Examples: (pg61)
1. The focus phoneme is /oa/, the focus grapheme is 'OA' and the chosen word is ***boat***.
The word /b/ – /oa/ – /t/ has three phonemes, with the focus phoneme in the middle.

2. The focus phoneme is /oa/, the focus grapheme is 'OW' and the chosen word is ***flown***.
The word /f/ – /l/ – /ow/ – /n/ has four phonemes, with the focus phoneme (somewhere) in the middle or more specifically the third sound that is heard.

You can then ask the students to think of other words which contains the focus phoneme. Don't worry if the words have a different grapheme (spelling). Example: toe, bone or open. Write their chosen words on the visual board, putting the words with the focus grapheme in one column, and words with alternative graphemes in another column. You can briefly talk about the differences between the graphemes in each of the columns. A simple statement to say is, "In this word, the sound /oa/ has a different spelling," or, "In this word, the letters (or digraph) 'OE' is represented by (or has) the sound /oa/." By doing this, the students are building a better understanding of the relationship between phonemes and graphemes. Remember to keep this relaxed and fun!

* * *

Create a set of flashcards, showing all the circle (●) graphemes and go through these daily, before focusing on the grapheme/phoneme of the day. As the square (■) graphemes are introduced, add these to your set of flashcards. Remember that a phoneme (sound) can be represented by different single letters or groups of letters (digraphs, trigraphs, quadgraphs) and a grapheme (letter) can be represented by different phonemes.

During lessons, it is very important to show lots of visual examples, as often as possible and to make sure that the students have a good understanding of each word. Introduce more new words gradually, using a mix of simple and challenging ones. Always explain the meaning of each new word, as they are introduced, giving examples in simple verbal or written sentences, showing clear pictures where possible.

Make up fun sentences using groups of words from the chosen word bank; this will help the student's memory and boost confidence.
Example: (pg60) The goat wore a coat on a boat.
Examples have been included at the top of each *MY NOTES* pages. Use this page to add your own fun sentences or to make general notes.

Future lessons may include checking whether the students can recall the list of words previously taught. Can they write down any of these words? Do they remember the meanings of the words? Are they able to identify digraphs, trigraphs, and quadgraphs within the words? Can they recite the fun sentences they had made up? Remember, repetition plays a crucial role in students' learning process. It is essential to provide your students with sufficient time to understand and fully grasp the new information being presented to them. Always praise their efforts and maintain a fun environment

When you feel the students are ready, or if it becomes relevant to their learning, you can introduce a new grapheme from the squares (■) word bank, for individual phonemes, eventually moving on to the diamonds (◆). Some words, in the diamond (◆) word bank, are quite obscure, so always focus on words that are relevant to the student's written and spoken language. Word banks are laid out alphabetically, within their colour coded groups, and are not in any specific order of learning. Remember that the Systematic Synthetic Phonics (SSP) programme you use may introduce alternative graphemes at different stages, or in a specific order.

You can focus on two or more graphemes for each phoneme at the same time. Choose words which the students are likely to use both verbally and in creative writing.
Example: (pg17) If the focus phoneme is /ai/, then the chosen graphemes can be as follows:
'AI'   – rain, train, wait
'AY'   – play, day, stay
'A-E'   – game, cake, name

Always write up your chosen words on a visual board, so that the students can see patterns in the words.

Some words can consist of more than one grapheme for the same phoneme. Throughout this book, the focus grapheme will be highlighted in **green** and the alternative grapheme, within the same word, will be highlighted in **black**.
Example: /s/ circus, sauce, saucy   /k/ clock, kick   /igh/ hindsight, identify, idolize

When adding suffixes to words, be aware of any changes made to the graphemes and phonemes.
Example: p-air and p-ai-r-i-ng   sh-are and sh-a-r-i-ng

Students may already be familiar with some, most, or all of the English alphabet. Reinforce this knowledge by teaching them the relationship between letter names and sounds, as well as the difference between 'spelling' and 'sounding out' a word. Encourage students to sound out high frequency words and practice how to spell them, as often as possible. Use a visual board for demonstrations, to help students better understand how a phoneme can be represented by different graphemes and how a grapheme can be represented by different phonemes.

A note on split vowel digraphs: While words such as *brute, rude, flute, rule*, etc., are often taught as a split vowel digraph, they are not 'true' split vowel digraphs. These words have the *long* /oo/ sound (pg65) instead of the /ue/ sound, as in *tube, mute, cube, amuse*, etc., (pg91). Words with both the *long* /oo/ and with the /ue/ sounds can indeed be taught at the same time, but it's important to organize the words into two columns, on a visual board, with a strong focus on the different phonemes. This will help students hear the difference between the two sounds.
Remember, a split vowel digraph is created when a long vowel digraph, which sounds like the name of its first letter and ends with an 'e', is split by a consonant (pg9).

* * *

Not every sound in a word or every word in a sentence is correctly stressed in our natural speech. Words can seemingly blend into each other, or parts of words can be omitted, altering how words within the sentence sound. It is vital to speak clearly and slowly, at first, before repeating the sentence at your natural speech pace. This is particularly important during dictation lessons and especially with very young students.
Example: *"This is for you."* can sound like '*Thi-siz fyou.*' and '*What are you doing?*' can sound like '*Wot-cha doing?*'

There are over 37 different British dialects and accents, which vary greatly across Great Britain, so special attention may be needed when teaching students who has a different dialect to yours. For instance, the words 'bath', 'castle' and 'laugh', are usually spoken with the /ar/ phoneme in Southern England, whilst spoken with the /a/ phoneme in parts of Northern England. These words will be found under the /ar/ phoneme (pg21). You may prefer to write these words on the 'My Notes' page under /a/ (pg15).

* * *

The length of some lists will vary, depending on the number of graphemes for each phoneme. Most words are only found once in this book, but some words can be found in two or more places, focussing on a different phoneme within that word.

The Graphemes to Phonemes word bank (pg106-123) contains the same words as the Phonemes to Graphemes word bank (pg14-105), although some lists may be much shorter. This book does not incorporate all potential graphemes for a given phoneme.

* * *

Throughout this reference book, make sure to highlight the words you have taught to your students. Jot down notes and add extra words, with the focus phoneme, to the *MY NOTES* pages. This will enable easy review and reinforcement of what you have previously taught.

Remember, there are 26 letters in the English alphabet, 44 phonemes and over 150 graphemes, which is quite a lot to learn, so always keep lessons relaxed and enjoyable! Bikoz teechin foniks shood orlwayz bee phun!!!

Miss Barrina

MY NOTES

The happy antelope and the angry alligator.
The man can catch the apple.

æ

Graphemes

● a	axe	crash	hanger	pant	stamp
accept	axis	dab	happen	pat	stand
act	back	dad	happy	patter	swam
acting	bad	daddy	hat	pram	tackle
active	badge	dagger	have	quack	tag
activity	bag	damage	jab	rack	tangle
actor	baggy	damp	jam	ramp	tango
add	band	dazzle	jazz	ran	tap
adhere	bang	dragon	ladder	rang	than
adjective	bangle	fact	lag	rant	thank
alligator	bank	fan	lamp	rat	that
alphabet	banker	fang	land	rattle	track
am	bat	fat	landing	relax	tragic
amber	battle	flag	lap	sack	tram
an	began	flat	mad	sad	tramp
and	black	gammon	magic	saddle	trample
anger	bland	gap	man	sand	trap
angry	blank	gas	manage	sang	travel
animals	cab	gash	mantle	sat	unhappy
animation	camera	gateau	map	Saturday	value
ant	camp	gather	marry	scab	van
antelope	can	glad	matter	scrap	vandalise
apple	candle	gnat	maxi	shall	wag
aqua	cap	gran	nag	slack	waggle
aquatic	carry	grand	nan	slam	wax
as	cash	grandad	nanny	slap	wrap
ash	cat	grandma	nap	snack	yak
at	catch	hammer	nappy	snag	yam
athlete	clap	hand	pack	snap	zap
atlas	crab	handle	paddle	span	◆ i
attack	crack	hang	pan	splat	meringue

MY NOTES

The snail left a trail of paint on my trainers.
Don't stray away, stay and play.

Graphemes

● ai				■ ay	sway	◆ ae
afraid	rail	cradle	flame	always	today	reggae
aid	rain	dangerous	game	array	tray	sundae
aim	rainbow	fable	gave	away	way	◆ aigh
bait	raise	famous	grape	bay	x-ray	straight
brail	reclaim	label	grave	clay	yesterday	straighten
brain	remain	lady	hate	crayon	■ ea	straighter
chain	sail	nation	lake	day	break	◆ ei
claim	snail	nature	lane	daytime	breaking	beige
complain	sprain	navel	late	decay	breakup	reiki
drain	stain	paper	made	delay	daybreak	reindeer
email	strain	stable	make	display	great	veil
explain	strainer	station	male	fray	greater	vein
fail	tail	strange	mate	lay	greatest	◆ et
faint	trail	stranger	name	May	steak	ballet
frail	train	table	page	okay	■ eigh	bouquet
gain	trainers	taste	place	pay	eight	buffet
grain	vain	tasty	plate	play	eighteen	crochet
hail	waist	waste	race	players	eighth	croquet
jail	wait		safe	playful	eighty	gourmet
maid	waiter	■ a-e	same	pray	flyweight	sachet
mail	■ a	ablaze	save	prayer	freight	sorbet
main	able	ate	shake	railway	neigh	◆ ey
maintain	ache	bake	shape	ray	neighbour	drey
nail	acorn	blame	skate	relay	outweigh	grey
paid	angel	brave	snake	replay	sleigh	obey
pain	apricot	cake	space	say	weigh	prey
paint	April	came	take	slay	weight	survey
painter	apron	cane	tale	spray	weighted	they
plain	baby	cave	trace	stay	weightless	
praise	bathe	date	wake	stray		
	cable	female	wave			
		flake				

MY NOTES

I sat on the ch*air* and brushed my h*air*.
Take c*are* not to st*are* at the squ*are*.

Graphemes

● air	fair	■ a	■ are	square	thereafter
air	fairness	area	aftercare	stare	thereby
airbag	flair	carer	**airfare**	tableware	therefore
airboat	funfair	caring	aware	unaware	where
airborne	hair	comparing	bare	wares	◆ ae
airbrush	hairball	glaring	barefoot	welfare	aerial
aircraft	hairbrush	parents	barely	■ ear	aerobics
aired	haircut	preparing	beware	bear	aeroplane
airfare	hairdo	scaring	care	eyewear	aerosol
airflow	hairdresser	scary	careful	footwear	aerospace
airless	hairless	sharing	careless	knitwear	◆ aire
airlift	hairnet	staring	childcare	neckwear	billionaire
airline	hairpin	varied	compares	nightwear	millionaire
airmail	hairstyle	various	cookware	outerwear	questionnaire
airport	highchair	vary	dare	overbear	trillionaire
airspace	impair	wariness	declare	pear	◆ ar
airstream	impairment	wary	fanfare	sportswear	scarce
airstrip	lair	■ ai	fare	swear	scarcely
airtight	midair	airily	flares	tear	scarcity
airtime	mohair	airiness	glare	wear	◆ eir
airwaves	pair	airing	hardware	wearproof	their
airway	paired	airy	hare	■ ere	theirs
armchair	pushchair	dairy	mare	anywhere	◆ hei
chair	repair	fairies	nightmare	compere	heiress
chairlift	stair	fairish	prepare	elsewhere	◆ heir
chairman	stairs	fairy	rare	everywhere	heir
debonair	stairway	fairyland	rarely	nowhere	heirdom
despair	unfair	hairy	scare	premiere	heirloom
disrepair	unfairly	pairing	share	somewhere	heirship
downstairs	upstairs	prairie	snare	there	
éclair	wheelchair		spare		

MY NOTES

A shark wore a scarf to the party in the dark.
Ask the staff to dance fast on the grass.

aː

Graphemes

● ar

ajar
alarm
alarming
arch
argue
arguing
ark
arm
army
art
artist
artistic
bar
barber
barge
bark
barking
barn
barter
car
card
cardigan
cargo
carpenter
carpet
cart
carton
cartoon
cartwheel
carve

char
charm
charming
chart
charted
dark
darken
darn
dart
far
farm
farmer
farmyard
fart
garden
gardening
garlic
hard
hardly
hark
harm
harmful
harp
harvest
jar
large
lark
marble
March
marching
mark

marker
market
parcel
parch
park
parking
part
partition
partner
party
remark
scar
scarf
scarves
shark
sharp
sharpener
smart
snarl
spark
sparkle
sparkly
star
start
starting
startle
starve
tar
target
varnish
yard

■ a

after
afterwards
answer
ask
banana
basket
bath
blast
branch
brass
cast
castle
chance
clasp
class
craft
crafty
daft
dance
dancer
draft
drama
fast
fasten
father
flask
gasp
ghastly
glance
glass

glasses
graph
grasp
grass
last
lava
mask
massage
master
nasty
pass
past
pastime
pasture
path
pathway
photograph
plant
planting
plaster
prance
pyjamas
raspberry
rather
sabotage
spa
staff
task
trance
unmask
vast

■ are

are

◆ ah

blah
hurrah

◆ al

balm
balmy
calf
calm
calming
calves
half
halves
palm

◆ au

aunt
aunty
draught
draughty
laugh
laughable
laughing
laughter

◆ ear

heart
hearth
heartily
heartless
hearty

MY NOTES

The **b**ig **b**oy put the **b**ent **b**at in the **b**lack **b**in.
The ro**bb**er stole a gru**bb**y pe**bb**le.

Graphemes

● b

able
about
above
absorb
airbag
baby
back
backed
backless
bad
badge
baffle
bag
baggy
bake
baked
bald
ball
balmy
ban
banana
bandage
bang
bangle
banned
banquet
bar
bark
barmy
barn

base
basket
bat
bath
bathe
battle
be
beach
beak
bear
beast
beauty
because
bed
bedroom
bee
beef
before
beg
began
behind
bell
below
bend
bent
best
bib
big
bike
bin
bird

birthday
biscuit
bit
black
bleed
blew
blink
blob
blow
board
boat
bob
book
boot
bop
bored
born
bother
bottle
bottled
bottom
bought
bow
box
boy
brag
brain
brave
bread
break
breakfast

bribe
brick
bride
bright
broke
broom
brother
brush
bucket
bud
bug
buggy
builder
building
bully
burger
burn
bus
bush
but
buzz
cabin
cable
celebrate
club
cob
crab
crumble
cub
cube
cubic

curb
double
drab
dustbin
elbow
fab
fabric
fibre
grab
habit
herb
hub
husband
jab
job
lab
lobes
marble
maybe
nimble
number
object
orbit
pub
public
rebel
reboot
robin
rub
scramble
slab

stub
stumble
sub
submarine
superb
tab
table
tablet
tribe
trouble
tub
tube
tumble
unbox
verbal
vibes
web
yob
zebra

● bb

bobbed
bobbin
bobbles
bubble
cabbage
cabby
clubbed
cobble
cobbler
dabble
dribble

ebbed
fibbed
gobble
grabbed
grubby
hobby
jabbed
jabbing
knobbly
lobbed
lobby
nibble
pebbles
quibble
rabbit
ribbon
robber
rubber
rubbery
rubbish
rubble
scabby
scrabble
scribble
shabby
slobber
squabble
stubble
tabby
webbed
wobble

MY NOTES

A cow ate corn at the picnic.
The quick chicken tried to trick the sick duck.

Graphemes

● c							◆ cqu
accent	clown	croak	buckle	shock	blink	strike	lacquer
accept	club	crook	cackle	sick	book	talk	racquet
acorn	clue	crop	chick	slack	break	thank	◆ kk
acting	clueless	cross	chicken	slick	broke	think	trekked
actual	coat	crow	chuck	smack	dark	wink	trekking
allergic	coin	crowd	chuckle	snack	fork	work	◆ qu
cab	cold	cub	click	socks	ink	◆ cc	bouquet
cactus	colourful	cube	clock	stack	keep	hiccup	conquer
cage	comb	cup	crack	stick	key	occasion	croquet
cake	come	cure	deck	sticker	kilt	occupy	lacquer
calf	comic	curly	dock	stock	kind	occur	marquee
call	conker	curry	duck	struck	king	soccer	mosquito
came	cook	custard	duckling	stuck	kiss	◆ ch	quay
camera	cooker	cut	flapjack	suck	kit	aching	quiche
can	cool	cute	flick	thick	kitten	chaos	quinoa
candle	corn	electric	gecko	thicker	market	chemist	tequila
cap	corner	epic	hack	tick	milk	choir	◆ que
cape	correct	logic	kick	ticket	oink	chord	antique
car	cosmic	mosaic	lick	track	park	chorus	boutique
card	cost	picnic	lock	trick	pink	echo	cheque
care	cot	plastic	luck	truck	prank	orchid	grotesque
cart	cotton	scab	muck	wicket	sank	psychic	mosque
cartoon	cough	strict	neck	wreck	shook	scheme	oblique
cat	count	sync	pack	yuck	sink	school	opaque
catch	cow	talc	pick	yucky	skate	stomach	physique
cave	crab	● ck	pickle	● k	sketch	◆ che	pique
clap	crawl	back	quack	ankle	skin	ache	plaque
clay	crayon	black	quick	bank	skip	headache	queue
clean	crazy	block	rack	bark	skirt	heartache	technique
cloud	cream	blocking	rock	beak	speak	toothache	unique
	creep	brick	sack	bleak	stalk		

MY NOTES

The tea**ch**er and **ch**ildren ate **ch**eese and **ch**ocolate.
Fe**tch** the ke**tch**up from the ki**tch**en.

Graphemes

● ch					◆ t	fetch
achieve	charred	childish	clench	pooch	actual	glitch
arch	chart	children	coach	porch	actually	hatch
attach	chat	chill	couch	pouch	adventure	hitch
attached	chatter	chilly	crouch	preach	capture	hutch
beach	cheap	chime	crunch	punch	factual	itchy
beech	cheaper	chimney	crunchy	punchline	fortunate	ketchup
belch	cheapest	chimp	detach	quench	fortune	kitchen
bench	cheat	chin	drench	ranch	future	latch
birch	cheater	chip	duchess	reach	gesture	match
blanch	cheating	chipped	each	research	lecture	matchstick
bleach	check	chippy	enrich	rich	misfortune	notch
branch	cheek	chive	finch	richer	natural	patch
brooch	cheeky	chocolate	flinch	riches	naturally	pitch
brunch	cheer	choice	highchair	roach	nature	pitcher
bunch	cheerful	choke	hunch	scorch	picture	rematch
bunches	cheers	choking	inch	search	unnatural	retch
chain	cheery	chomp	launch	speech	venture	satchel
chair	cheese	choose	leech	squelch		scratch
chalk	cheesy	choosing	lunch	such	◆ tch	sketch
champ	cheque	chop	lunchtime	teach	batch	snatch
chance	chequer	chopper	lurch	teacher	bewitch	snitch
change	cherry	chore	March	torch	blotch	splotch
chap	chess	chose	marching	torched	botch	stitch
chapel	chest	chosen	much	touch	butcher	stretch
chapter	chew	chuck	mulch	touched	catch	swatch
char	chewing	chuckle	munch	trench	clutch	switch
charge	chewy	chum	ouch	wheelchair	crutch	thatch
charger	chick	chunky	peach	which	despatch	twitch
charm	chicken	church	perch	◆ c	ditch	watch
charming	chief	churn	pinch	cellist	etch	witch
	child	chutney	poach	cello		

MY NOTES

Did the dog dig a hole in my bed?
I will cuddle my teddy in the muddy puddle.

Graphemes

● d

adult
adventure
advise
aid
and
bad
band
bandage
bed
bedroom
bend
beside
bird
blend
blood
board
body
bond
bud
build
building
card
cloud
cod
code
cord
crowd
dad
daily
dam

damage
dark
darling
date
day
dear
deep
deer
den
desk
dew
did
dig
dim
dip
dipping
dirty
disappoint
dish
display
dive
do
dog
doing
done
donkey
dot
double
drain
dream
dress

dressing
drier
drink
drip
drop
dry
dug
end
field
found
friend
glad
good
goodbye
grand
ground
had
hand
handle
hard
harden
hardly
herd
hold
hurdle
kid
laid
land
lead
led
lend

loud
mad
made
mend
Monday
paid
pod
pond
pound
pride
proud
radio
read
record
red
ride
sad
sadly
said
send
slid
slide
sold
spend
stand
stride
Sunday
toad
today
wand
word

● dd

add
addictive
addition
address
bedding
bladder
buddies
caddy
cuddle
daddy
haddock
hidden
huddle
kidding
ladder
madden
middle
muddle
muddy
nodd**ed**
odd
oddest
paddle
paddling
peddle
prodding
pudding
puddle
redden
sadden

saddle
shredding
skidding
sudden
teddy
toddler
udder

■ ed

banged
banned
begged
bobbed
breathed
claimed
cleared
crawled
darkened
drained
fanned
frayed
ingrained
joined
opened
played
prayed
rolled
sprayed
stayed
strayed
swayed
turned

■ ed

ashamed
craved
damaged
dyed
grazed
lived
loved
moved
praised
pu**dd**led
raised
saved
tied
used

■ ed

(/i/ + /d/) see pg45

addicted
boarded
bonded
granted
pounded
recorded

■ *ed*

(/t/) see pg83

brushed
cracked
finished
jumped
laughed
talked

MY NOTES

I will s**e**ll the **e**gg and the p**e**ncil for a p**e**nny.
I dr**ea**mt of a h**ea**lthy br**ea**kfast in the m**ea**dow.

Graphemes

● e				■ ai	heavy	◆ a
bed	every	mental	slept	again	instead	any
bell	excited	mention	smell	against	jealous	anybody
belt	February	net	smelt	said	lead	anyhow
bend	fell	never	spell	unsaid	leant	anymore
bent	felt	next	spend		leapt	anyone
best	fetch	pen	step	■ ea	leather	anything
bet	fled	pencil	stress	ahead	meadow	anytime
better	flesh	penny	tell	already	meant	anyway
clever	forget	pepper	ten	bread	measure	anywhere
correct	fresh	pest	tennis	breakfast	pleasure	many
den	fret	pet	terrible	breast	read	manyfold
dental	gentle	plentiful	test	breath	ready	◆ ei
dentist	get	plenty	text	breathless	realm	heifer
depend	held	present	them	cleanse	spread	leisure
desk	help	press	then	dead	stead	leisurely
develop	helpless	pretend	trend	deadly	steady	◆ eo
dress	hen	protect	very	deaf	stealth	jeopardize
edge	jet	quest	vet	deafening	sweat	jeopardy
education	kept	question	welcome	dealt	sweater	leopard
egg	left	record	well	death	sweaty	◆ ie
electric	leg	red	went	dread	thread	befriend
elephant	lend	rent	west	dreamt	threat	boyfriend
else	length	rest	wet	feather	tread	friend
empty	less	sell	when	feathery	treasure	girlfriend
end	lesson	send	whenever	head	unhealthy	unfriendly
enemy	let	sent	yellow	headset	wealth	◆ u
enjoy	letter	set	yelp	health	wealthy	burial
enter	medal	shelf	yes	healthy	weapon	buried
entrance	medicine	shell	yet	heather	weather	bury
ever	melt	shelves	zen	heaven	zealous	
	men	sketch	zest			

I cleared the earwax from my ear, now I can hear.
The deer drank beer and was cheerful.

Graphemes

● ear
appear
appeared
arrears
beard
bearded
clear
cleared
clearly
dear
dearly
disappear
ear
earache
eardrop
eardrum
earlobe
earplug
earring
earwax
earwig
endear
fear
feared
fearless
gear
geared
hear
linear
near
nearby

nearly
reappear
rear
reared
rears
sear
shear
sheared
smear
smeared
spear
speared
tear
tearful
tears
year
yearly

■ eer
auctioneer
beer
career
cheer
cheerful
deer
domineer
engineer
jeer
leer
peer
pioneer
puppeteer

queer
reindeer
sheer
sneer
steer
veer
volunteer

◆ e
era

◆ ea
appearance
appearing
clearing
dearest
hearing
idea
nearest
nearing
shearing
smearing
teary
wearily
weary

◆ ee
cheering
domineering
eerie
eerily
engineering
jeering

steering
veering

◆ ei
madeira

◆ eir
weird
weirdest
weirdly
weirdo

◆ ere
adhere
here
hereby
interfere
severe
severely
sincere
sincerely
sphere
werewolf

◆ ier
cashier
fierce
fiercely
frontier
pier
pierce
piercing
tier
tierce

MY NOTES

The green sheep had three teeth.
I believe that the thief stole the shield.

Graphemes

● ee	queen	he	bean	steal	fifty	◆ eo
agree	reef	me	beast	steam	funny	people
asleep	see	neon	breathe	stream	happy	◆ i
bee	seed	scenery	clean	tea	jelly	antique
beef	seek	scenic	cream	teacher	lady	boutique
bleed	seem	she	dream	team	lazy	machine
breeze	seen	we	each	treat	lorry	mosquito
cheek	sheep	■ e-e	easel	weak	party	physique
cheese	sheet	athlete	easy	wheat	pony	police
creep	sleep	compete	eat	■ ey₁	pretty	quiche
deep	sleet	complete	heal	key	silly	quinoa
eel	sleeve	concrete	heat	off-key	sorry	sardine
feed	speed	delete	ideal	ley	sunny	◆ ie
feel	street	eve	leaf	■ ey₂	tidy	believe
feet	sweep	evening	leak	alley	tiny	brief
fifteen	sweet	extreme	leap	chimney	twenty	chief
flee	teen	extremely	meal	donkey	very	field
free	teeth	obese	meat	journey	windy	frieze
freeze	three	obsolete	peace	money	◆ ae	grief
geese	tree	precede	peach	monkey	algae	niece
greed	weed	recede	peanut	ropey	larvae	piece
green	week	scene	peas	turkey	◆ ay	priest
greet	weep	swede	please	valley	quay	relief
heel	wheelchair	theme	preach	■ y	◆ ei	shield
keep	■ e	these	reach	bunny	ceiling	shriek
knee	be	trapeze	read	busy	deceive	thief
kneecap	demon	■ ea	real	carry	receipt	◆ oe
meet	emu	beach	sea	city	receive	coeliac
need	equal	bead	seal	crazy	seize	diarrhoea
peel	even	beak	seat	family	seizure	phoenix
peep	female		speak			
			squeak			

The ey2 and y graphemes, both have a slightly shorter /ee/ sound.

MY NOTES

The mermaid gave her the perfect gerbil.
I got a shirt for my thirteenth birthday.

/er/

Graphemes

● er

alert
concern
deserve
dessert
deter
divert
expert
expertly
external
fern
fertile
gerbil
germ
her
herb
herbal
herd
kerb
mercy
merge
mermaid
merman
nerve
nervous
nervously
observe
observer
perch
perfect
perk

perky
perm
person
personal
preserve
refer
reserved
reverse
serve
service
stern
swerve
term
terminal
termly
thermal
universe
university
verb
verbal
verse
vertical
vertigo

■ ere

were

■ ir

affirm
birch
bird
birth

birthday
chirp
chirpy
circle
circuit
circular
circus
confirm
dirt
dirty
fir
firm
firmly
first
girl
irk
quirky
shirt
sir
skirt
smirk
squirm
squirt
stir
swirl
third
thirst
thirsty
thirteen
thirteenth
thirty

twirl
twirp
whirl

■ or

artwork
legwork
network
word
wordy
work
worker
workman
workout
world
worldly
worm
wormery
worse
worship
worst
worth
worthy

■ ur

blur
blurb
blurt
burden
burger
burglar
burn

burning
burnt
burp
burst
church
churn
curb
curd
curfew
curl
curling
curly
cursive
cursor
curtain
curve
disturb
fur
furl
furlong
furnish
furniture
furry
further
gurgle
gurney
hurdle
hurl
hurt
hurtful
incur

lurch
lurk
murky
nurse
nursery
occur
purge
purl
purple
purse
recur
return
slur
slurp
slurping
spurt
sturdy
surf
surface
surge
surgeon
surgery
surgical
surname
surplus
Thursday
turban
turf
turkey
turn
turned
turner

turnip
turtle
urban
urge
urgent
urn
yurt

◆ ear

earl
early
earn
earnest
earth
earthling
heard
hearse
learn
overheard
pearl
rehearse
research
researcher
search
unearth
unheard
unlearn
yearns

◆ our

adjourn
journal
journey

MY NOTES

A fairy did a fart on the funny sofa.
The dolphin played the saxophone down the telephone.

A fairy did a fart on the funny sofa.
The dolphin played the saxophone down the telephone.

f

Graphemes

● f				● ff	puffer	morph
after	fetch	foil	frozen	affect	puffy	nephew
beef	few	fold	fruit	affirm	raffle	nymph
calf	field	follow	fry	affix	rebuff	paragraph
craft	fifteen	food	fun	afford	ruffle	phantom
daft	fifty	fool	funny	baffle	scoff	phase
deaf	fight	foot	fuse	bluff	scruffy	phew
fab	fill	for	gifted	buffer	shuffle	phlegm
face	filler	force	golf	buffet	sniff	phobia
faint	find	forest	half	cliff	staff	phone
fairy	finger	forgive	knife	coffee	stiff	phoneme
fall	finish	forgot	leaf	coffin	stuff	phonics
false	firm	fork	left	cuff	stuffy	phony
family	first	forty	life	differ	suffer	photo
fan	fish	foul	lift	different	suffix	photocopy
far	fit	found	loaf	effect	tariff	photograph
fare	five	four	loft	effort	toffee	phrase
farm	fix	fourteen	nifty	fluff	waffle	physical
farmer	flag	fox	often	fluffy	whiff	physics
fart	flake	frail	proof	giraffe		saxophone
fast	flask	free	raft	gruff	▪ ph	sphere
fasten	flavour	freeze	reef	guffaw	alpha	telephone
fat	flea	fresh	refer	huff	alphabet	trophy
father	flew	fret	rife	muffin	aphids	◆ gh
fault	float	Friday	sofa	muffle	autograph	cough
feather	flock	friend	soft	off	dolphin	enough
feed	flood	fright	strife	offend	elephant	laugh
feel	floor	frog	thrifty	offer	epiphany	laughter
feet	flow	from	trifle	office	graph	rough
fell	flower	front	wafer	officer	grapheme	tough
fern	flown	frown	wife	puff	humph	trough
	fog	froze	wolf		lymph	

MY NOTES

The alligator and the dragon said goodbye to the grumpy pig.
The juggler begged the smuggler for an egg.

Graphemes

● g

again
ago
agree
alligator
anger
angular
argue
argument
bag
beg
big
brag
brigade
bug
burger
clog
dig
disagree
disgust
dog
drag
dragon
earwig
engage
finger
flag
fog
forget
forgiven
forgotten
frog
gag
gain
game
gap
garden
gas
gate
gather
gave
gay
gaze
gear
get
gift
gifted
girl
give
given
glad
glare
glass
glitter
global
globe
glow
go
goal
goalie
gold
golden
golf
good
goose
gorilla
gown
grab
grace
graceful
grand
grant
grape
grasp
grass
graze
grease
greasy
greedy
grief
grim
grin
grip
groan
ground
group
grout
grove
grow
growl
grown
grumpy
gull
gully
gulp
gum
gurgle
gushed
gust
gusty
gut
gutter
guy
guzzle
hungry
igloo
jigsaw
jungle
leg
legal
magnet
mug
nag
pagan
peg
pig
pigsty
rag
rig
rug
rugby
seagull
signal
single
singular
stag
swig
tangle
tog
twig
ugly
wig

● gg

aggressive
baggage
baggy
beggar
begged
bigger
boggy
buggy
dagger
digger
egg
eggcup
foggy
giggle
goggle
groggy
haggle
jiggle
jogger
jogging
juggle
juggler
lagging
legged
luggage
maggot
muggy
niggle
nugget
pegged
rigged
saggy
shaggy
sluggish
smuggler
snuggle
soggy
stagger
struggle
tagged
toggle
trigger
twiggy
wiggle
wriggly
zigged

◆ gh

aghast
ghastly
gherkin
ghost
ghosting

◆ gu

guarantee
guess
guests
guidance
guide
guidebook
guilt
guilty
guise
guitar

◆ gue

analogue
catalogue
colleague
dialogue
fatigue
intrigue
league
morgue
plague
prologue
rogue
vague
vogue

◆ x

(/g/+/z/)
see pg103

exact
exam
example

MY NOTES

The **h**ungry **h**amster ate the **h**uge **h**amburger.
Whose is the **wh**olesome **wh**olemeal?

Graphemes

● h

behave	happen	heap	hexagon	hoop	hungry
childhood	happiness	hear	hi	hop	hunt
greenhouse	happy	heard	hibernate	hope	hurdle
habit	harass	heart	hidden	hopeful	hurry
had	hard	hearty	hide	horizon	hurt
haddock	hardly	heat	high	horn	husky
haggle	hare	heater	highest	horrible	hustle
hail	harm	heath	hike	horrid	hut
hair	harmful	heave	hiker	horrify	hutch
hairball	harmony	heaven	hill	horsefly	hydrate
hairbrush	harness	heavy	him	hose	hype
hairy	harp	hedge	himself	hosepipe	hyper
half	harsh	heel	hinge	hospital	perhaps
halfway	harvest	height	hint	hospitality	somehow
hall	has	held	hip	hot	unhappily
hallway	hat	helicopter	hippo	hotter	unhappy
halt	hatch	hell	hired	house	unhurt
halves	hate	hello	hiss	housefly	upheld
ham	haunt	help	history	household	withheld
hamburger	have	helper	hit	how	withhold
hammer	hawk	helpless	hobby	however	
hammock	hay	hem	hockey	howl	**◆ wh**
hamper	haystack	hen	hog	hub	
hamster	hazard	henna	hold	huddle	who
hand	hazardous	her	hole	hug	whoever
handle	he	herb	holiday	huge	whole
handy	head	herd	home	hum	wholemeal
hang	headed	here	homeless	human	wholesale
hanger	heady	hermit	honey	humble	wholesome
haphazard	heal	hero	hood	hunch	wholly
	healthy	hers	hook	hundred	whom
					whose
					whosoever

MY NOTES

The prince took a drink of milk inside the igloo.
The orange package is in the palace.

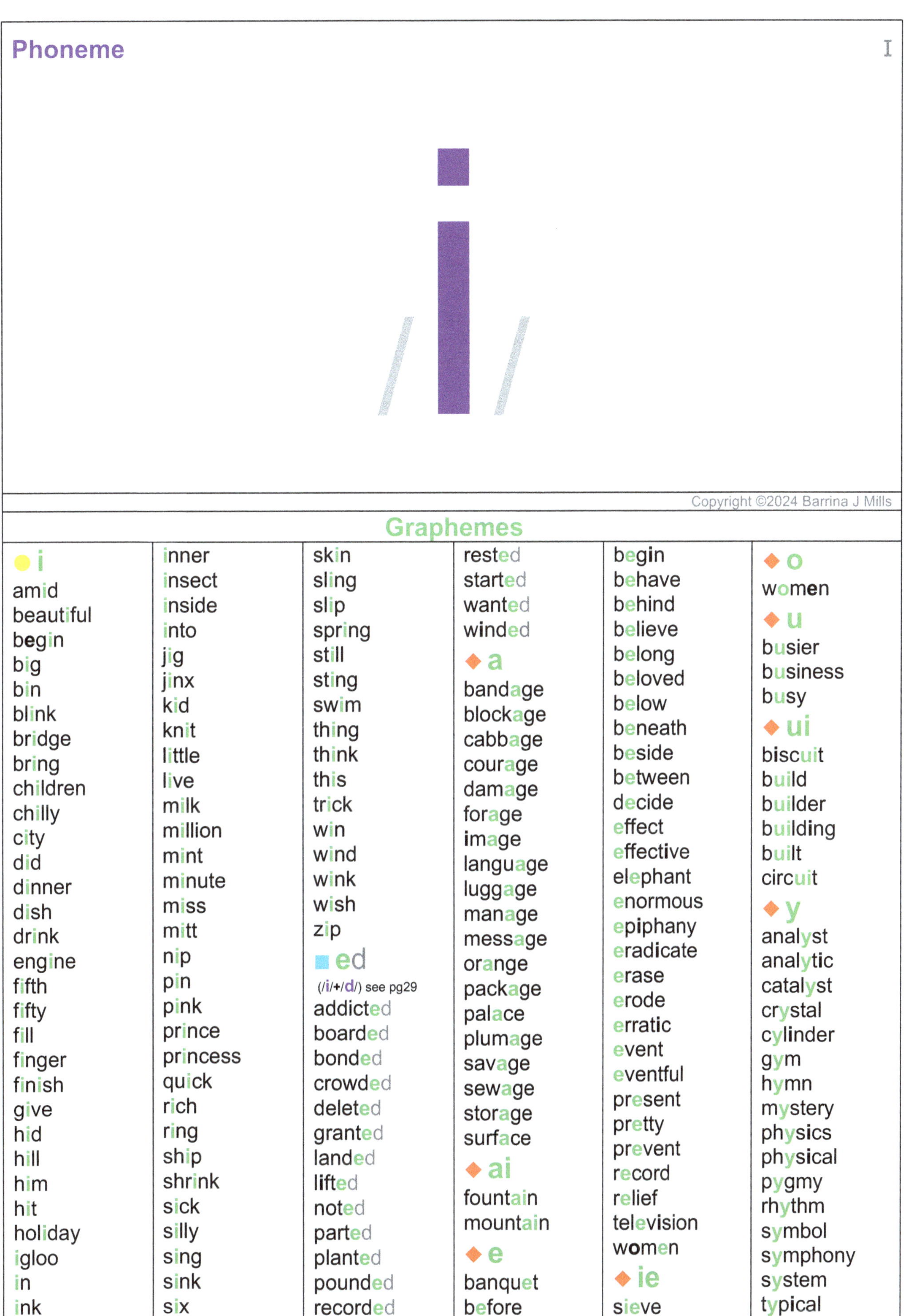

Graphemes

● **i**

amid
beautiful
begin
big
bin
blink
bridge
bring
children
chilly
city
did
dinner
dish
drink
engine
fifth
fifty
fill
finger
finish
give
hid
hill
him
hit
holiday
igloo
in
ink

inner
insect
inside
into
jig
jinx
kid
knit
little
live
milk
million
mint
minute
miss
mitt
nip
pin
pink
prince
princess
quick
rich
ring
ship
shrink
sick
silly
sing
sink
six

skin
sling
slip
spring
still
sting
swim
thing
think
this
trick
win
wind
wink
wish
zip

■ **ed**

(/i/+/d/) see pg29

addicted
boarded
bonded
crowded
deleted
granted
landed
lifted
noted
parted
planted
pounded
recorded

rested
started
wanted
winded

◆ **a**

bandage
blockage
cabbage
courage
damage
forage
image
language
luggage
manage
message
orange
package
palace
plumage
savage
sewage
storage
surface

◆ **ai**

fountain
mountain

◆ **e**

banquet
before

begin
behave
behind
believe
belong
beloved
below
beneath
beside
between
decide
effect
effective
elephant
enormous
epiphany
eradicate
erase
erode
erratic
event
eventful
present
pretty
prevent
record
relief
television
women

◆ **ie**

sieve

◆ **o**

women

◆ **u**

busier
business
busy

◆ **ui**

biscuit
build
builder
building
built
circuit

◆ **y**

analyst
analytic
catalyst
crystal
cylinder
gym
hymn
mystery
physics
physical
pygmy
rhythm
symbol
symphony
system
typical

MY NOTES

At n**igh**t the l**igh**tning gave me an alm**igh**ty fr**igh**t!
Wh**y** did the sh**y** sp**y** cr**y**?

igh

/ igh /

Copyright ©2024 Barrina J Mills

Graphemes

● igh		eye	i-e	ie	y	◆ ais / ei / eigh / i	more

● igh
airtight
bright
daylight
delight
delightful
fight
flight
flightless
fright
frighten
high
highchair
highest
highlight
insight
knight
light
lightning
lighter
midnight
might
nigh
night
nightfall
nightlife
right
sigh
sight
sightings
slight

spotlight
thigh
tight
tighten
tonight
upright
uptight

■ eye
eye
eyebrow
eyelash
eyelet
eyelid
eyesight

■ i-e
alive
arrive
beside
bike
bite
bitesize
dive
drive
fine
five
hide
ice
inside
invite
knife

life
like
line
live
mice
mile
mine
nice
nine
outside
pile
pipe
polite
price
prize
provide
quite
rice
ride
rife
ripe
shine
side
site
size
smile
spice
stride
strife
strike
stripe

surprise
survive
time
twice
while
white
wide
wipe
wise
write

■ ie
classifies
complies
cried
cries
denies
die
died
dies
dried
dries
flies
fried
fries
implies
lie
lies
outflies
pie
replies
skies
specifies

spied
spies
supplies
tie
ties
tried
tries
untie

■ y
by
cry
deny
dry
fly
fry
imply
July
my
myself
outcry
pry
reply
rhyme
shy
sky
sly
spy
sty
supply
try
why

◆ ais
aisle

◆ ei
eider
eiderdown
either
neither

◆ eigh
height
heighten
sleight

◆ i
behind
blind
child
find
Friday
grind
hindsight
I
idea
ideal
identify
identity
idolize
kind
library
mild
mind
minute

private
remind
science
silence
sizes
spider
tidy
title
violence
wild
wind
writer

◆ ir
fire
firefly
fireside
iron
wire
wireless

◆ is
island
islander
isle

◆ uy
buy
buyer
guy

◆ ye
bye
goodbye

MY NOTES

We jump and jiggle to joyful jazz!
The vengeful surgeon used a strange orange bandage.

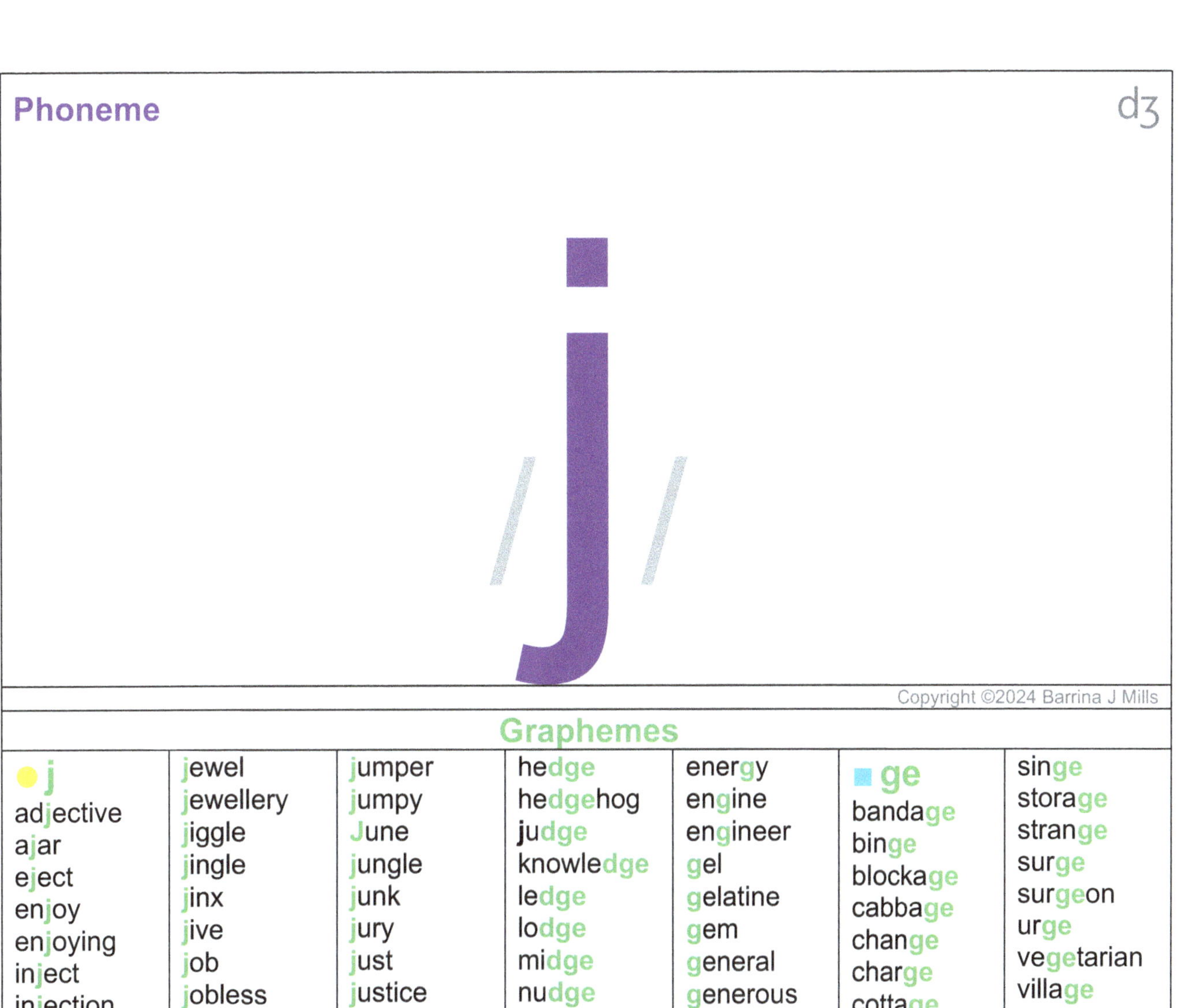

Graphemes

● j

adjective
ajar
eject
enjoy
enjoying
inject
injection
injure
injury
jab
jacket
jade
jaded
jaguar
jail
jam
January
jar
jargon
jaunt
jaw
jay
jazz
jean
jeep
jeer
jelly
jellyfish
jest
jet

jewel
jewellery
jiggle
jingle
jinx
jive
job
jobless
jog
jogger
join
joint
joke
joker
jolly
jolt
jot
journal
journey
joy
joyful
judge
judo
jug
juggle
jugular
juice
juicy
July
jumble
jump

jumper
jumpy
June
jungle
junk
jury
just
justice
jut
juvenile
majority
object
objected
objection
reject
rejection
subject
unjust

■ dge

abridge
badge
bridge
budge
dodge
dredge
drudge
edge
fledge
fridge
fudge
grudge

hedge
hedgehog
judge
knowledge
ledge
lodge
midge
nudge
pledge
porridge
ridge
sledge
sludge
smidge
smudge
stodge
trudge
wedge

■ g

age
allergic
apologize
astrology
badger
cage
danger
dangerous
detergent
digit
emergency
energise

energy
engine
engineer
gel
gelatine
gem
general
generous
gentle
gerbil
germ
giant
gigantic
gin
ginger
gingerly
giraffe
gym
imagine
magic
magical
margin
origin
page
rage
rigid
stage
stranger
teenager
tragic
urgent

■ ge

bandage
binge
blockage
cabbage
change
charge
cottage
courage
cringe
damage
forage
forge
fringe
garbage
hinge
huge
image
language
large
luggage
manage
orange
package
plumage
purge
range
ravage
revenge
savage
sewage

singe
storage
strange
surge
surgeon
urge
vegetarian
village
voyage

◆ ch

ostrich
sandwich
spinach

◆ d

educate
graduate
graduation
individual
procedure
soldier

◆ dj

adjacent
adjective
adjoin
adjourn
adjust

◆ gg

exaggerate
suggest
veggie

MY NOTES

The lovely lamb lay on my lap.
Fill the ball with yellow jelly.

/l/

Graphemes

● l

alive
along
April
black
blood
blow
cheerful
clever
clock
coil
control
cool
crawl
curl
daily
deal
feel
flask
flood
flower
foil
frail
gerbil
girl
growl
ideal
island
label
lace
laid

lamb
land
landing
lap
large
laugh
law
lawn
lay
layer
lazy
learn
led
leg
less
lesson
let
lettuce
lick
lid
light
like
lip
listen
lit
live
loaf
lobby
lock
log
lonely

long
look
loose
lose
lot
loud
love
lovely
low
lower
loyal
luck
lung
mail
meal
melon
owl
pearl
pencil
plain
plan
plenty
police
pool
prowl
quilt
slack
slap
slim
solid
spoil

● ll

allow
ball
balloon
bell
belly
bill
brilliant
brolly
bull
bully
call
chill
collar
controller
doll
drill
fall
falling
fell
fill
follow
football
frill
full
grill
hall
hello
hill
jelly
jolly

kill
lollipop
lolly
mellow
pill
pillar
pillow
pull
quill
roll
roller
sell
shall
silly
skill
small
smell
stall
still
swallow
swell
tall
tally
tell
telly
trolley
wall
well
will
yell
yellow

■ le₁

aisle
freestyle
gargoyle
hairstyle
isle
lifestyle
restyle
style
voile

■ le₂

(/uh/ then /l/)
also see pg93

able
angle
ankle
apple
bicycle
bubble
buckle
cable
candle
circle
cobble
couple
crumble
cycle
dazzle
eagle
edible
giggle

goggle
grumble
humble
juggle
jumble
jungle
kettle
middle
muddle
mumble
needle
noodle
pebble
pickle
puddle
purple
puzzle
recycle
simple
single
snuggle
stable
startle
struggle
stumble
table
tackle
tickle
trouble
tumble
uncle

MY NOTES

The mermaid ate a magic mini mango.
Simmer the yummy gammon in summer.

Graphemes

● m

aim
alarm
almighty
almost
animal
arm
boom
bottom
broom
charm
charming
compare
cream
creamy
dime
domino
dream
employ
enjoyment
enormous
exam
family
famous
farm
germ
gym
ham
hem
him
improve
jam
mad
magic
mail
maintain
make
male
man
mango
many
map
march
mark
mask
massive
master
mat
May
maybe
me
meal
mean
meet
melon
member
memory
men
mermaid
merman
mess
met
midnight
might
mighty
mildew
milk
mime
mind
mine
mini
mirror
miss
mist
model
modern
moist
moisture
Monday
money
monster
month
moon
mop
mope
mother
mould
mount
mouse
mouth
movement
movie
mow
much
muesli
mug
mule
mum
music
must
mute
my
mystery
myth
name
number
palm
plum
problem
ram
remember
room
smack
small
storm
stream
sum
swamp
swim
team
tomboy
tram
uniform
warm

● mm

ammonia
comma
command
comment
commit
common
dilemma
dimmed
drummer
dummy
gammon
gimmick
grammar
gummy
hammer
hammock
hemmed
hummed
immerge
immune
jammy
jimmy
mammal
mammoth
mummify
mummy
plummet
rummage
scammer
scummy
shimmer
shimmy
simmer
skimmed
summary
summer
summit
summon
swimmer
tummy
yummy

◼ me

awesome
become
come
enzyme
fearsome
gruesome
handsome
income
irksome
loathsome
lonesome
outcome
overcome
regime
some
tiresome
twosome
welcome
wholesome

◆ gm

diaphragm
paradigm
phlegm

◆ mb

bomb
climb
comb
crumb
dumb
honeycomb
lamb
limb
numb
outclimb
plumb
plumber
succumb
thumb
tomb
upclimb
womb

◆ mn

autumn
column
condemn
damn
hymn
limn
solemn

MY NOTES

Enjoy the fun clown.
The knackered knight had a knobbly knee.

Phoneme

/n/

Graphemes

● n		north	snail	● nn	swanning	◆ gn
again	grown	nose	snap	annexe	tenner	align
an	human	not	snot	annoy	tennis	alignment
ant	in	note	snow	annual	thinner	assign
any	kitchen	nothing	soon	banner	tunnel	benign
ban	lawn	noun	spin	beginner	winner	campaign
barn	learn	now	spoon	bonnet		design
been	man	ocean	sprain	bunny	■ kn	feign
begin	moon	often	stern	cannot	knack	foreign
bun	nag	own	stone	conned	knackered	foreigner
burn	name	paint	sun	dinner	knave	gnarl
can	nap	pant	swan	fennel	knead	gnarly
churn	nasty	pen	ten	flannel	knee	gnash
clean	nature	pencil	then	funnel	kneecap	gnat
clown	near	person	thin	funny	kneel	gnaw
coin	nearly	piano	tin	henna	knelt	gnome
corn	need	plain	tint	inner	knew	gnomic
den	needle	plane	tonight	innocent	knife	gnomish
down	neon	poison	town	kennel	knight	gnosis
earn	nerve	punch	train	manners	knit	gnu
engine	nest	punish	turn	nanny	knives	malign
enjoy	net	quaint	twin	penny	knob	realign
fern	never	queen	under	pinned	knobbly	reign
flown	new	rain	unicorn	planner	knock	resign
frown	next	rant	warn	punnet	knoll	sign
fun	nice	reindeer	when	runner	knot	◆ pn
garden	night	rent	won	runny	know	pneuma
grain	nil	return	wonder	scanned	knowledge	pneumatic
gran	nine	run	wonderful	scanner	known	pneumonia
green	nod	sewn	worn	spinner	knows	pneumonic
groan	noon	shown	yawn	sunny	knuckle	
					unknown	

MY NOTES

Going fishing in the morning!
Lick the meringue with your tongue!

ŋ

ng

/ng/

Graphemes

• ng						
adding	costing	gang	outing	smiling	wrong	hungry
along	craving	going	packing	song	wrongly	ink
amazing	crying	gong	peeling	sprang	yawning	jungle
amazingly	cuddling	grasping	peering	sprung	young	junk
among	cycling	growing	ping	sting	younger	link
bang	dancing	hang	playing	stinging	zing	mango
banging	digging	hanger	pong	stopping	◆ n	monk
barking	ding	hanging	pudding	string	anger	oink
being	doing	humming	pulling	stroking	angle	pink
belong	dong	hung	pushing	strong	angler	prank
biting	drawing	icing	quaking	strung	angry	rank
bling	drilling	jogging	rang	stung	ankle	rink
blocking	dropping	joining	recycling	stunning	anxiety	sank
blowing	drumming	juggling	rhyming	sung	anxious	shrink
boing	duckling	jumping	ring	swing	bank	shrunk
boomerang	eating	kicking	ringing	swinging	bankrupt	single
boxing	enjoying	king	rung	swirling	banquet	sink
bring	evening	kingdom	running	swung	blank	skunk
bringing	exciting	knowing	sang	thing	blanket	stink
building	falling	knowingly	shaking	tong	blink	tango
buzzing	fang	landing	shining	topping	bunk	tank
calling	farming	learning	sing	twang	clink	thank
cheering	filming	liking	singer	undoing	conker	think
clang	finding	long	singing	voting	crank	twinkle
climbing	fishing	looking	sinking	waking	donkey	uncle
cling	fling	lying	sipping	warning	drink	wink
clocking	floating	marching	sitting	wedding	finger	wrinkle
clung	flowing	morning	skipping	whining	frank	◆ ngue
coming	flying	needing	slang	wing	fungal	meringue
cooling	following	nothing	sleeping	wring	honk	tongue
	furlong	opening	sling	wringing	hunger	tongueless

MY NOTES

The frog fell off the box.
I'm watching the swan in the swamp.

Phoneme

Graphemes

● o

across	crockery	jog	opposite	snot	swan
along	crop	knock	opt	snotty	swap
block	cross	knot	option	socks	swat
blot	crossed	lobby	orange	soft	waffle
body	dock	lock	orangutan	softly	waft
bog	dog	locker	oxygen	song	wallet
borrow	dot	locket	plot	sorry	wand
bottle	dotted	log	plotted	spot	wander
bottom	drop	long	pocket	stock	want
bottomless	dropper	longing	pop	stop	was
box	flock	lost	popper	stopper	wash
boxer	fob	lot	possible	strong	washer
boxing	fog	mock	pot	swot	wasp
cannot	foggy	model	potty	tog	watch
chocolate	follow	modern	probably	toggle	what
chop	forest	monster	problem	top	whatever
clock	forgot	mop	produce	topper	whatnot
cloth	fox	not	promise	topple	
coffee	frock	object	proper	trot	**◆ ach**
cog	frog	October	rob	upon	yacht
comma	from	octopus	robber	wrong	yachting
common	god	odd	rock	yonder	yachtsman
compare	golf	of	rockery		yachtswoman
computer	gone	off	rocket	**■ a**	
control	got	offence	rot	quad	**◆ au**
copper	hobby	offer	shock	quality	because
copy	hog	office	shop	quarrel	sausage
cost	hop	often	shopping	squad	
costly	hospital	on	shot	squash	**◆ ou**
cot	hot	opera	slot	swab	cough
	job	opinion	smock	swallow	coughed
				swamp	coughing
					trough

MY NOTES

The goat wore a coat on a boat.
The crow had flown below the rainbow.

əʊ

Graphemes

● oa	o	obedient	cove	throne	owner	dominoes
boast	soap	oboe	doze	vote	pillow	echoes
boat	stoat	ocean	drove	whole	rainbow	foe
bloat	throat	October	froze	woke	shadow	forgoes
cloak	toad	old	globe	wrote	shallow	goes
coach	toast	olden	grove	zone	show	hoe
coal	toaster	older	hole		shown	oboe
coast		only	home	■ ow	slow	roe
coat	■ o	open	hope	arrow	snow	sloe
coax	ago	over	hose	below	sow	tiptoe
croak	bold	photo	joke	blow	throw	toe
float	both	poem	lobe	blown	tomorrow	toenail
foal	cargo	poet	lone	borrow	tow	woe
foam	clothes	poetry	lonely	bow	window	woeful
goal	cold	radio	mole	bowl	yellow	◆ oo
goalie	comb	so	nose	crow		brooch
goat	domino	sofa	ozone	elbow	◆ au	brooches
groan	don't	told	phone	flow	chauffeur	◆ ou
hoax	echo	total	poke	flown	mauve	bouquet
load	fold	won't	pole	follow	◆ eau	mould
loaf	go	yo-yo	remote	glow	bureau	poultry
loan	gold	■ o-e	rope	grow	gateau	shoulder
moan	golden	alone	rose	grown	plateau	soul
oak	hello	bone	slope	know	◆ ew	soulful
oats	hold	broke	smoke	known	sew	◆ ough
poach	hotel	choke	spoke	low	sewn	although
road	mobile	chose	stone	lower	◆ oe	dough
roam	moment	clone	strobe	marrow	aloe	doughnut
roast	moped	close	stroke	meadow	cargoes	furlough
shoal	most	cone	telephone	mow	dingoes	though
soak	no	cope	those	narrow	doe	
	notice			own		
	November					

MY NOTES

Don't sp**oi**l the **oi**l with p**oi**son.
The r**oy**al cowb**oy** is enj**oy**ing the v**oy**age.

Graphemes

● oi

adenoid	groin	pointing	■ oy
adjoin	hoist	pointy	ahoy
android	join	poise	alloy
anoint	joined	poison	annoy
anointed	joiner	poisonous	annoying
appoint	joining	quoit	bellboy
appointed	joint	recoil	boy
appointment	jointly	rejoice	boycott
avoid	joist	rejoin	boyhood
avoided	koi	roils	boyish
avoidance	loin	sirloin	buoy
boil	loiter	soil	buoyancy
boiler	meteoroid	soiled	convoy
boiling	moist	spoil	corduroy
boing	moisten	spoiled	cowboy
boisterous	moisture	spoiler	coy
broil	moisturize	spoilt	coyly
choice	noise	tabloid	coyness
coil	noisier	thyroid	decoy
coiling	noisiest	toil	deploy
coin	noisy	toilet	destroy
coinage	oil	toiletries	destroyed
cuboid	oily	turmoil	disemploy
devoid	oink	turquoise	disloyal
doily	ointment	uncoil	employ
embroider	paranoia	unspoiled	employer
embroidery	paranoid	voice	employment
embroil	pinpoint	voiceless	enjoy
foil	point	void	enjoyable
goiter	pointed	voided	enjoying
	pointer	voile	enjoyment

envoy
flamboyant
foyer
joy
joyful
joyfully
joyless
joyous
joyously
joyride
killjoy
loyal
loyally
loyalty
overjoy
oyster
pageboy
ploy
royal
royalty
soy
soybean
tomboy
toy
toying
toyshop
unemployed
unjoyful
unroyal
voyage
voyager

MY NOTES

Let's z**oo**m to sch**oo**l on a sc**oo**ter.
The br**ui**sed fr**ui**t on the cr**ui**se was s**ui**table to make j**ui**ce.

Graphemes

● oo			▪ o	flume	◆ ou
achoo	igloo	snoop	drew	flute	group
aloof	kangaroo	snooty	flew	include	route
balloon	kazoo	snooze	grew	June	router
bamboo	loo	soon	jewellery	parachute	soup
bathroom	loom	sooner	outgrew	prune	wound
bedroom	loop	sooth	screw	rude	wounded
bloom	moo	soothing	sewage	rule	◆ ough
boom	mooch	spook	threw	salute	through
boost	mood	spool	unscrew	▪ ue	throughout
boot	moon	spoon	withdrew	blue	◆ u
booth	noodle	stool	▪ o	clue	plumage
broom	noon	swoop	do	cruel	ruin
cartoon	oodles	taboo	disprove	glue	ruler
choose	ooze	tattoo	improve	sue	ruling
coo	oozing	teaspoon	lose	true	truly
cool	poo	too	move	▪ wo	truth
cooler	pooch	tool	movie	two	truthful
cooling	pool	toot	prove	twofold	unruly
doom	proof	tooth	remove	twos	◆ ui
drool	roof	toothless	tomb	twosome	bruise
droop	room	troop	who	◆ oe	cruise
food	roomy	woozy	whom	canoe	fruit
fool	root	zoo	womb	canoeing	fruitful
foolish	school	zoom	▪ u-e	shoe	fruity
goose	scoop	zooming	absolute	shoebox	juice
groove	scooper	▪ ew	brute	shoehorn	juicy
hoof	scoot	blew	chute	shoelace	suit
hoop	scooter	brew	elude	shoestring	suitable
hoot	shampoo	chew	exclude	shoetree	unsuitable
hooves	shoot	chewed	fluke		
	smooth	crew			

MY NOTES

The woodpecker likes to look at a good book.
The bully pushed and pulled the butcher.

Graphemes

🟡 **oo**

afoot
book
bookable
bookcase
booking
bookish
booklet
brook
cook
cooker
cookery
cookies
crook
crooked
deadwood
fishhook
foot
footage
football
footballer
footer
footing
footless
footman
footy
good
goodbye
goodness
goods
hood

hooded
hoodie
hook
hooligan
hooray
look
looking
lookout
mistook
nook
oomph
oops
outlook
overlook
overtook
plywood
prebook
rebook
retook
rook
rookie
shook
snood
soot
sooty
stood
swoosh
took
uncooked
understood
unhook

vroom
whoopee
whoosh
wood
wooden
woodpecker
woody
woof
wool
woollen
woolly

🟦 **u**

bull
bullet
bulletin
bullion
bullish
bullock
bully
bullying
bulrush
bush
bushy
butcher
butchery
cushion
cushy
fulfil
full
fully
output

pudding
pull
pulley
push
pushchair
pushy
put
putting
sugar
sugary

🔶 **o**

werewolf
wolf
wolfish
woman
womanhood
womanly

🔶 **oul**

could
could've
couldn't
couldn't've
should
should've
shouldn't
shouldn't've
would
would've
wouldn't
wouldn't've

MY NOTES

The short stork ate a corn in the morning.
I caught my daughter being naughty, so I taught her the right way.

Graphemes

● or

adorn
afford
born
chord
cor
cord
cordial
cork
corn
corner
dorm
for
fork
form
fort
forty
gorm
horn
horse
lord
morning
north
or
orb
order
porch
pork
port
scorch
short
snorkel
snort
sort
sport
stork
storm
stormy
sword
sworn
thorn
torch
torn
worn

■ a

all
almost
alright
although
always
bald
ball
call
fall
false
hall
halt
salt
scald
small
stall
tall
wall
water
wrath

■ al

beanstalk
chalk
sleepwalk
stalk
talk
walk

■ au

applause
astronaut
August
aura
author
auto
autumn
cause
fault
faulty
haunt
launch
laundry
maul
pause
sauce
sauna
taunt
taut

■ augh

caught
daughter
naughty
taught

■ aw

awful
awkward
awning
bawl
brawl
claw
crawl
dawdle
dawn
draw
drawn
fawn
flaw
gnaw
hacksaw
hawk
jaw
law
lawn
paw
prawn
raw
saw
sawdust
sawn
shawl
spawn
sprawl
straw
thaw
trawl
trawler
withdraw
yawn

■ o

boring
snoring
storage
story
storyteller

■ oor

door
doorway
floor
poor
poorly

◆ ar

award
dwarf
quarter
reward
swarm
war
wardrobe

wards
warm
warmth
warn
warp

◆ aur

dinosaur

◆ oa

abroad
broad
broaden

◆ oar

aboard
boar
boarding
boards
coarse
hoard
hoarder
hoarse
oars
roar
soar
uproar

◆ ore

ashore
before
bore
core
explore

more
ore
pore
score
shore
snore
store
swore
tore
wore

◆ ough

bought
brought
fought
nought
ought
sought
thought
wrought

◆ our

course
court
courtyard
four
fourth
mourn
pour
sourced
your
yourself

MY NOTES

The mouse ran around outside the house.
Don't drown the flower with a powerful shower.

Graphemes

● ou

abound
about
account
aloud
amount
announce
around
astound
blackout
blouse
bounce
bouncy
bound
boundary
bounded
bout
cloud
cloudy
couch
council
count
counter
countess
counting
clout
crouch
cutout
discount
dismount
doubt

encounter
foul
found
founder
fountain
ground
grounded
grounding
grouse
grout
hound
house
housing
joust
jouster
loud
louder
loudest
loudly
lounge
louse
lousy
miscount
mount
mountain
mouse
mousy
mouth
mouthy
noun
ouch

ounce
out
outbid
outburst
outdoor
outer
outfit
outing
outlandish
outlet
outside
outsider
pouch
pound
pout
pouting
pronoun
proud
proudly
recount
round
rounders
rouse
scout
scrounge
shout
shouted
slouch
snout
sound
soundless

south
spouse
sprout
stout
surround
thou
thousand
tout
trousers
trout
unfounded
vouch
voucher
without
workout
wound

■ ow

allow
allowed
anyhow
bow
brow
brown
brownie
browse
clown
clowning
cow
coward
cowslip
crowd

crowded
crown
crowned
disallow
dowel
down
downer
downhill
downside
downy
drown
drowsy
empower
flower
flowering
fowl
frown
frowned
frowning
gown
growl
how
however
howl
meow
now
nowt
owl
plow
powder
powdery

power
powerful
prowl
prowler
scowl
shower
showery
somehow
sow
towel
tower
town
trowel
vow
vowel
wow

◆ ho

hour
hourly

◆ o

flour
our
ourself
scour
sour

◆ ough

bough
drought
plough
slough

MY NOTES

My pet pig ate purple pasta.
I popped the stroppy kipper into a wrapper.

Graphemes

● p		p			● pp	
alp	limp	pen	poor	separate	app	popper
ape	lips	penny	pop	September	appear	poppy
apricot	mop	people	pork	shape	apple	puppet
April	nap	perfect	pot	sharp	apply	puppy
asleep	nip	perfume	potato	ship	approve	rapper
bleep	open	person	pound	simple	choppy	ripped
cap	pack	pet	pour	sip	clapping	ripple
cheap	page	pick	pout	slap	copper	sapped
computer	paid	pie	press	sleep	crappy	shipped
creep	paint	piece	pretty	slip	crippled	shopped
creepy	pair	pig	price	splat	cropped	shopping
crop	pan	pine	pride	stamp	cuppa	slipper
cup	pant	pink	prince	step	dipper	slippy
deep	park	pip	princess	stomp	disappear	sloppy
depart	part	pirate	prize	stop	drippy	soppy
depend	parting	place	proud	strip	dropped	stopper
drop	party	plank	prove	stripe	flappy	stopping
empty	pass	plant	prowl	super	floppy	stroppy
equip	passport	plaster	prune	swap	happen	supper
flap	past	plate	pudding	swoop	happily	supply
flip	pasta	play	pull	tap	happy	support
gap	pat	player	pulp	top	hippie	swapped
grip	path	please	pup	trap	hippo	tapping
hip	pause	plenty	pupil	trip	kipper	topper
jeep	paw	plum	purple	triple	lippy	topping
jump	pea	point	purse	turnip	mapping	topple
keep	peace	police	put	viper	nappy	tripped
kept	pear	polite	reap	wasp	nippy	upper
kip	pearl	pond	ripe	whip	pepper	wrapper
lamp	peas	poo	ripen	wipe	popped	yippee
	peg	pool	scrape	zip		zipper

MY NOTES

Quickly squeeze the square squirrel.
The queen is quiet and tranquil.

Graphemes

● qu

aqua	quail	quiff	squat
aquarium	quaint	quill	squatter
aquatic	quake	quilt	squawk
aqueous	qualify	quilted	squeak
banquet	quality	quilting	squeaky
conquest	quantum	quin	squeal
earthquake	quarrel	quince	squeamish
enquire	quarry	quip	squeeze
equal	quart	quirk	squelch
equality	quarter	quirky	squid
equalizer	quartet	quit	squint
equate	quartz	quite	squire
equation	quash	quitter	squirm
equator	quaver	quiver	squirrel
equinox	queasy	quiz	squirt
equip	queen	quoit	squish
equipment	queenly	quota	squishy
equity	queer	quotation	tranquil
equivalent	quench	quote	tranquillity
exquisite	query	quoted	turquoise
frequent	quest	quotes	unequal
infrequent	question	request	**◆ cqu**
inquest	quibble	require	acquaint
inquiry	quick	requirement	acquaintance
liquefy	quicken	sequel	acquainted
liquid	quickly	sequence	acquirable
quack	quicksand	sequin	acquire
quad	quickstep	squad	acquired
quadruple	quid	squalor	acquiree
quads	quiet	square	acquit
	quieten	squash	acquitted

MY NOTES

The brave rabbit ran around the rat.
The squirrel saw a raspberry lorry.

Graphemes

● **r**

around	raincoat	return	rough	
brave	raise	reward	round	
brick	ram	rib	row	
brim	ramp	ribbon	royal	
bring	ran	rich	rub	
brown	rang	rid	rubber	
crack	range	riddle	rude	
creep	rant	ride	ruin	
cricket	rare	rig	rumour	
crisps	rat	right	run	
cry	rate	rim	runner	
dairy	rather	ring	scram	
dress	raw	rinse	scrap	
drill	ray	riot	sprint	
drum	read	rip	sprout	
entry	ready	ripe	strong	
fairy	reap	ripple	syrup	
forest	reboot	river	throat	
from	record	road	track	
grant	red	roar	tractor	
green	rejoice	roast	train	
hairy	relax	rob	trainer	
print	remain	robber	tram	
prod	remember	robin	trap	
rabbit	rep	rock	tray	
race	repair	rode	treat	
rack	rescue	room	tree	
rag	research	rope	trick	
rain	rest	rose	trip	
rainbow	restful	rot	triple	
	result	rotten	try	

● **rr**

array	porridge
arrear	quarrel
arrest	quarry
arrival	raspberry
arrive	scurry
arrow	sorrow
barrel	sorry
barrier	sparrow
berry	squirrel
blueberry	starry
borrow	strawberry
burrow	surround
carrot	terror
carry	warrior
cherry	worry
correct	yarrow
curry	
error	
farrow	
ferry	
furry	
horrid	
hurry	
irregular	
lorry	
marry	
merry	
mirror	
narrow	
parrot	

■ **wr**

enwrap	wriggle
rewrite	wriggly
unwrap	wrings
wrap	wrinkle
wrapper	wrinkly
wraps	wrist
wrath	writ
wreath	write
wreck	writer
wreckage	writing
wren	written
wrench	wrong
wrestle	wrongly
wretch	wrote
	wrought
	wrung

◆ **rh**

rhapsody
rhetoric
rhetorical
rheumatic
rhinestone
rhino
rhinoceros
rhomboid
rhubarb
rhyme
rhyming
rhythm
rhythmic
rhythmist

MY NOTES

The **s**mall **s**tar **s**parkle in **s**pace.
The hor**se** was let loo**se** in the hou**se**.

Phoneme

Graphemes

● s

atlas
best
biscuit
bus
cost
desk
dust
east
famous
forest
insect
inside
opposite
plastic
question
sachet
sack
sad
saddle
sail
sale
sand
Saturday
say
seat
see
sell
send
set
several

sick
side
sigh
sing
sink
sip
sit
size
slap
sleep
slide
slip
slow
slurp
small
soap
soil
sold
song
soon
soot
sort
sound
soup
space
spare
sparkle
speak
spoil
spoon
sport

spotty
sprain
spray
spread
spring
spy
stand
star
stare
start
statue
steak
stir
stone
stood
straight
straw
street
study
sudden
Sunday
sunny
surname
swallow
swear
sweat
swede
sweet
swirl
swore
taste

test
vest
wasp
west
yes
zest

● ss

across
address
boss
brass
dress
essence
fossil
fuss
grass
hiss
kiss
less
mess
miss
pass
press
sass

■ c

accent
accept
access
bicycle
ceiling

celery
cell
cement
centimetre
centipede
cinema
cipher
circus
city
cycle
dancer
December
medicine
pencil
princess
recipe
saucy
specific
spicy
vaccinate

■ ce

chance
dance
essence
fence
glance
juice
justice
lettuce
office
palace

peace
pence
piece
police
pounce
practice
prance
prince
sauce
saucepan
sentence
silence
since
space
voice

■ se

cease
course
decease
else
horse
house
loose
mouse
purse
release
rinse

■ st

castle
fasten

glisten
jostle
listen
listening
thistle
whistle

◆ ps

psych
psychic
psycho
psychology

◆ sc

fascinate
muscle
scenario
scene
scenery
scenic
scent
scented
science
scissors

◆ sw

answer
sword
swordfish

◆ z

blitz
quartz
waltz

MY NOTES

Did the goldfish shout at the shabby shark?
Don't mention the addition section.

/sh/

Graphemes

● sh				◆ ch	◆ si	detention
afresh	goldfish	shave	shower	chandelier	conversion	direction
ash	gushed	shawl	shown	chef	dimension	edition
ashamed	hairbrush	she	shriek	chute	expansion	emotion
awash	harsh	shear	shrink	machine	extension	emotional
banish	hush	sheep	shrivel	parachute	mansion	eruption
bash	jellyfish	sheer	shrug	**◆ che**	pension	fiction
blush	lash	sheet	shuffle	cache	tension	fraction
brush	mash	shelf	shush	crèche	**◆ ss**	friction
bush	mesh	shell	shut	moustache	assurance	intention
bushy	mushroom	shield	shy	niche	assure	junction
cash	polish	shift	smash	quiche	pressure	lotion
cashew	posh	shimmer	splash	**◆ ci**	reassure	mention
cashier	punish	shimmy	squash	artificial	tissue	motion
clash	push	shin	squeamish	delicious	**◆ ssi**	nation
crash	quash	shine	squish	especially	compression	option
crush	rash	ship	stash	facial	discussion	optional
cushion	relish	shirt	swish	gracious	mission	petition
dash	reshape	shock	tarnish	musician	passion	portion
dish	rush	shoe	trash	official	permission	potion
earshot	shabby	shook	trashed	optician	**◆ ti**	ration
eyelash	shade	shoot	usher	precious	action	rotation
finished	shading	shop	vanish	social	addition	section
fish	shadow	shopping	wash	special	affection	sedation
fishing	shaggy	shore	washer	vicious	ambition	selection
flash	shake	short	wish	**◆ s**	attention	sensation
flesh	shall	should	wishful	insurance	caution	sensational
foolish	shame	shoulder	worship	sugar	contortion	solution
fresh	shape	shout	**◆ ce**	sure	dedication	station
gash	share	shove	liquorice	surely	deletion	stationary
gnash	shark	shovel	ocean			stationery
	sharp	show				

MY NOTES

He puff**ed** and cough**ed** when he jump**ed**.
Ge**t** fi**t** firs**t**!

Graphemes

● t						
accept	jet	snot	tree	button	splatter	sacked
act	kilt	stir	trip	dotty	tattoo	stacked
active	kit	stop	truth	fatter	tatty	talked
actor	let	swat	turn	fatty	twitter	tapped
ant	master	sweet	tweak	flitter	watt	touched
bit	mat	table	twist	grotto		trapped
bite	meet	take	urgent	gutter	■ ed	watched
bright	net	talk	vent	kettle	backed	wrecked
built	next	tap	vest	kitten	blessed	
cat	opt	taxi	vet	matt	blocked	■ te
cot	out	tea	waist	matter	brushed	baste
count	paint	teach	wait	mitt	chipped	caste
dot	past	tear	waiter	mitten	coughed	distaste
dirt	pat	teat	wet	motto	cracked	haste
dirty	plaster	teeth	what	mutter	cramped	paste
event	plot	tell	white	natter	crushed	reroute
exit	post	ten	wit	nettle	dipped	route
feet	pot	tennis	yet	nutty	dropped	suite
fight	potato	tense	yoghurt	pattern	finished	taste
first	quest	test	zest	patty	fixed	waste
fit	quit	tiger		petty	hooked	◆ bt
foot	rent	time	● tt	pitta	jumped	debt
get	rest	toilet	attach	potty	kicked	doubt
gift	roast	told	attempt	pretty	laughed	misdoubt
goat	seat	total	battle	putt	linked	redoubt
great	select	toy	better	putty	marched	subtle
greet	sent	trace	bitten	rattle	marked	◆ pt
hat	set	tram	bitter	settee	mixed	nonreceipt
host	shut	trap	bottle	shutter	parked	receipt
hot	sit	tray	bottom	sitter	peaked	◆ th
	smart	treat	boycott	sitting	puffed	thyme
			butter		ripped	

MY NOTES

My father and brother wore the smoothest clothing.
They'd rather go bathing together.

Phoneme

Graphemes

● **th** voiced

al**th**ough	sli**th**er	**th**ose
ano**th**er	smoo**th**	**th**ou
ba**th**ing	smoo**th**est	**th**ough
boo**th**	smoo**th**ie	**th**us
bo**th**er	soo**th**ing	**th**y
brea**th**ing	tee**th**ing	**th**yself
bro**th**er	te**th**er	toge**th**er
bro**th**erly	**th**an	unwor**th**y
clo**th**ing	**th**at	wea**th**er
ei**th**er	**th**e	wea**th**erman
fa**th**er	**th**ee	wea**th**erproof
fa**th**erly	**th**eir	whe**th**er
fea**th**er	**th**eirs	wi**th**
fea**th**ery	**th**em	wi**th**draw
fur**th**er	**th**emselves	wi**th**er
ga**th**er	**th**en	wi**th**in
ga**th**ering	**th**ence	wi**th**out
hea**th**er	**th**enceforth	wi**th**stand
la**th**er	**th**ere	wor**th**y
lea**th**er	**th**ereabouts	■ **the**
lea**th**ery	**th**ereafter	ba**the**
loa**th**ing	**th**ereby	brea**the**
mo**th**er	**th**erefore	clo**the**
mo**th**erly	**th**erein	la**the**
nei**th**er	**th**ereof	loa**the**
o**th**er	**th**ereon	sca**the**
o**th**erwise	**th**ereupon	see**the**
ra**th**er	**th**ese	soo**the**
rhy**th**m	**th**ey	sunba**the**
rhy**th**mic	**th**ine	tee**the**
	this	unclo**the**

The a**th**lete **th**ought she came four**th**.
The warm**th** made the you**th** **th**irsty.

θ

Graphemes

● **th** unvoiced

amethyst	fifth	panther	thickener	throat
anthem	filth	path	thief	throb
anything	footpath	pathway	thigh	throne
athlete	forth	pith	thimble	through
athletic	froth	plinth	thin	throw
author	frothy	python	thing	thrown
authorise	girth	seventh	think	thud
bath	goth	sixth	third	thumb
bathrobe	growth	sloth	thirsty	thump
bathtub	hath	something	thirteen	thunder
beneath	health	sooth	thirty	Thursday
birth	healthy	south	thistle	thwart
birthday	hearth	strength	thorn	thyroid
both	length	sympathy	thorny	tooth
breath	lengthy	teeth	thorough	toothache
broth	lethargy	tenth	thoroughly	toothbrush
cloth	loath	thank	thought	toothpaste
death	mammoth	thankful	thoughtful	toothpick
depth	marathon	thanks	thoughtless	toothy
earth	maths	thaw	thousand	truth
earthlike	method	theatre	thrash	truthful
earthly	month	theme	thread	twelfth
earthy	monthly	theory	threat	underneath
eighth	moth	therapeutic	threaten	warmth
eleventh	mouth	therapy	three	wealth
empath	myth	thermal	threw	wealthy
empathy	mythical	thermometer	thrift	worth
ethical	ninth	thermos	thrifty	wrath
ethnic	north	thesaurus	thrill	wreath
faith	nothing	thick	thriller	youth
	oath	thicken	thrive	youthful

MY NOTES

You must shuffle under the umbrella.
The young couple had enough of the country.

Λ

Graphemes

● **u**

begun	husband	result	unbutton	cover	stomach
blunt	hut	rubber	uncle	coverage	ton
blush	insult	run	under	done	**u**ndercover
brush	jug	runner	undermine	dove	**u**nd**o**ne
bump	jump	rush	underneath	dozen	won
bun	jumper	shuffle	understand	front	wonder
bunk	junk	shun	undone	glove	worry
bus	just	shut	undress	govern	
but	jut	skull	unlike	honey	■ **oo**
butter	luck	structure	unpack	love	blood
button	lucky	strut	up	lovely	flood
buzz	lump	stuck	upcoming	Monday	
club	lunch	study	update	money	◆ **oe**
cup	much	stun	uphill	monk	does
cupboard	muck	such	uplift	monkey	doesn't
cut	mud	sudden	upmost	month	
drum	mug	suddenly	upon	monthly	◆ **ou**
duck	munch	summer	upset	mother	country
dull	muslin	sun	upsetting	none	couple
dust	must	Sunday	us	nonetheless	cousin
flush	numb	sunk		nothing	double
fun	number	sunlight	■ **o**	onion	enormous
funny	public	sunny	above	other	enough
fuss	publication	truck	another	otherwise	nourish
gum	publish	trust	brother	oven	nourishment
gun	publisher	tusk	colour	shove	rough
hum	pump	ugly	colourful	shovel	touch
hundred	pun	ulcer	come	smother	touchy
hungry	punch	umbrella	comfort	some	tough
hurry	punish	unable	comfortable	someone	trouble
	putt	unblock	company	son	young
			compass		youngest
					youngster

Don't arg**ue** in the que**ue** on **Tue**sday.
The c**ute** d**uke** **use** perf**ume**.

Graphemes

● **ue**
argue
autocue
avenue
barbecue
continue
cue
due
endue
hue
issue
miscue
muesli
overdue
pursue
queue
rescue
residue
revenue
statue
subdue
tissue
Tuesday
undue
value
venue
virtue

■ **ew**
anew
curfew
dew

dewy
few
fewer
knew
mew
mildew
nephew
new
newbie
news
newt
pew
phew
renew
renewal
skew
skewer
spew
stew
stewing

■ **u**
dual
duality
duel
duo
duty
fuel
fuelled
future
human
humanity

menu
music
musical
musician
pupil
refuel
reunited
student
stupid
unicorn
uniform
unify
union
unique
unit
unite
united
universal
universe
university
unusual
usual
usually

■ **u-e**
amuse
amusement
assume
bemuse
confuse
consume
costume

cube
cute
duke
excuse
fume
fuse
huge
introduce
misuse
mule
mute
nude
perfume
produce
reduce
refuse
reproduce
retune
reuse
tube
tune
use
useful
volume

◆ **eau**
beaut
beautician
beautiful
beautifully
beautify
beauty

◆ **eu**
eucalyptus
euphemism
feud
feudal
neutral
neutralize
neutron
pneumatic
pneumonia
pseudonym

◆ **iew**
interview
overview
preview
review
view
viewable
viewer
viewfinder
viewless
viewpoint

◆ **uu**
vacuum
vacuumed

◆ **you**
you
youth
youthen
youthful

The teacher stuck a plaster on the dancer in winter.
The woman ate a special pizza.

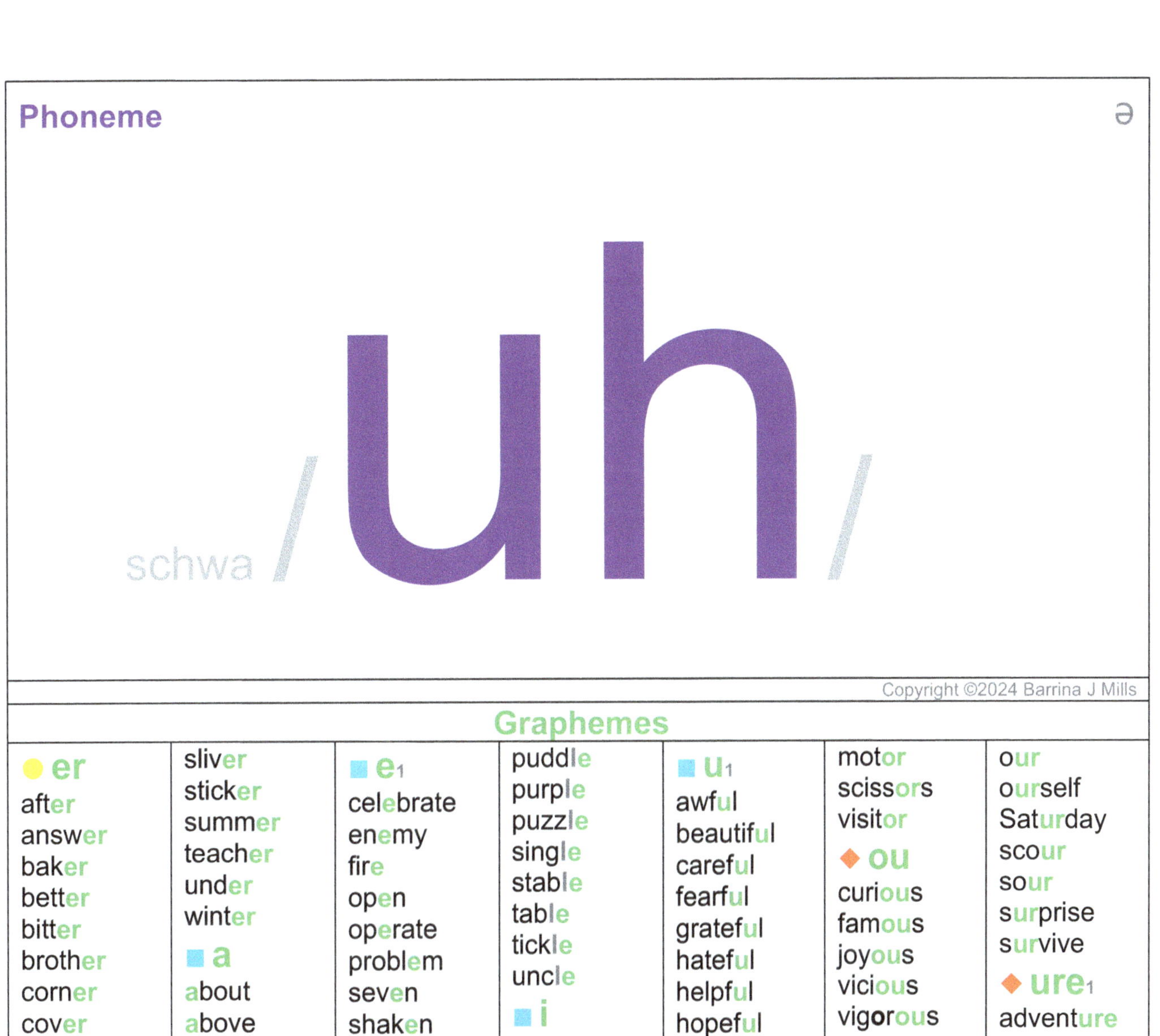

Graphemes

● er
after
answer
baker
better
bitter
brother
corner
cover
dancer
dinner
ever
farmer
father
flower
hamster
letter
litter
lower
mister
monster
mother
never
over
paper
plaster
power
printer
river
silver
sister

sliver
sticker
summer
teacher
under
winter

■ a
about
above
across
address
afraid
allow
amaze
amount
animal
apply
around
balloon
banana
capable
elephant
equal
opera
pedal
pizza
several
special
via
vitamin
woman

■ e₁
celebrate
enemy
fire
open
operate
problem
seven
shaken
taken
the
towel
wire

■ le₂
(/uh/ then /l/)
also see pg51
ankle
apple
bicycle
bubble
buckle
candle
circle
giggle
grumble
juggle
kettle
middle
needle
noodle
pebble

puddle
purple
puzzle
single
stable
table
tickle
uncle

■ i
April
family
incredible
invisible
pencil
stencil

■ o
bottom
confront
dinosaur
dozen
eloquent
history
nation
occur
oppose
other
parrot
ration
today
tomorrow
tonight

■ u₁
awful
beautiful
careful
fearful
grateful
hateful
helpful
hopeful
joyful
lawful
mindful
playful
tearful
thankful
useful

◆ ar
collar
leopard
pillar
popular
similar
solar
sugar
vinegar

◆ or
actor
alligator
doctor
minor

motor
scissors
visitor

◆ ou
curious
famous
joyous
vicious
vigorous

◆ ough
borough
thorough

◆ our
armour
colour
favour
flavour
neighbour
odour
rigour
rumour
savour
vigour

◆ u₂
focus
supplier
supply

◆ ur
flour
hour

our
ourself
Saturday
scour
sour
surprise
survive

◆ ure₁
adventure
capture
closure
figure
future
gesture
injure
lecture
measure
nature
picture
pleasure

◆ ure₂
(s/oo/ +/uh/)
immature
mature ◆

ure₃
(/y/+ s/oo/ +/uh/)
cure
insecure
obscure
pure
secure

The e1, e2, i and u1 graphemes, have a slightly weaker schwa /uh/ sound.

MY NOTES

Would you ever be brave in a cave?
Have the nerve to forgive!

Graphemes

● v				■ f	live
activity	forgave	seventy	verb	of	loaves
adventure	gave	severe	verse	thereof	love
alive	govern	shave	version	whereof	motive
brave	grave	shovel	very		move
caravan	gravy	silver	vest	■ ve	nerve
cave	grove	skive	vet	above	olive
cavern	hive	slave	vetted	active	passive
chive	hover	sliver	vex	approve	prove
clever	invent	stove	victim	believe	receive
clover	invest	survey	vile	calves	relieve
cover	invisible	television	villa	captive	remove
crave	jive	travel	vine	creative	shove
creativity	knave	trivial	vinegar	curve	sieve
diva	knives	valley	violet	deceive	sleeve
dive	lives	value	violin	delve	solve
drive	movie	van	viper	deserve	starve
driven	nervous	vanish	virtue	dove	swerve
eve	oven	variety	visible	eave	valve
even	over	vary	vision	eaves	waive
evening	overly	vast	visit	elves	weave
event	pave	veal	visitor	evolve	wolves
eventful	prevent	veer	vital	forgive	
ever	private	vegan	vitamin	give	◆ vv
every	provide	veil	vixen	glove	divvy
favour	quaver	vein	voice	grieve	divvying
favourite	quiver	velvet	void	halves	revved
fever	reveal	vengeance	vomit	have	revving
feverish	reverend	venison	wave	heave	savvier
five	river	venom	wavy	leave	savviest
flavour	seven	vent	wove	leaves	savvy
	seventeen	ventilate	woven		skivvy

We watch the waiter swim away.
Why did the whale whip the wheel?

Phoneme

Graphemes

● w

awake
award
aware
away
awoke
between
beware
reward
rewind
swam
swan
swap
swat
sway
sweat
swede
sweet
swell
swelter
swerve
swim
swing
swirl
towel
tweak
twelve
twenty
twin
twirl
twist

twit
wade
waffle
wag
waist
wait
waiter
wake
walk
wall
waltz
wand
wander
want
wanted
war
wardrobe
wards
warm
warn
warrior
was
wash
wasp
watch
water
watering
wave
wax
waxy
way

wayward
we
weak
wealth
wean
wear
weather
weave
web
wedding
weed
week
weekend
weep
weigh
weight
weird
weirdo
welcome
welfare
well
went
wept
were
west
wet
wig
wiggle
win
winch
wind

wing
wink
winner
winter
wisdom
wise
wish
witch
with
withheld
withhold
within
wobble
woe
woke
wolf
woman
won
wonder
wonderful
wood
wooden
wool
woolen
word
wore
work
worker
world
worm
worn

worry
worship
worst
worth
worthy
would
woven
wriggle

■ o

(/w/ + /u/)

once
one
oneness
oneself
onesie

■ wh

anywhere
awhile
elsewhere
everywhere
nowhere
somewhere
whack
whale
what
whatever
wheat
wheel
wheeze
when

whenever
where
whereas
whet
whether
which
while
whilst
whim
whimp
whimper
whines
whinge
whip
whiplash
whirl
whisk
whisker
whisper
whistle
white
whitewash
whittle
whizz
whoa
whoop
whopper
why

◆ u

language
penguin

MY NOTES

The pixie and the fox fixed the luxury box.
The boxer in the tuxedo relax to the saxophone.

Graphemes

● **x**

affix
axel
axis
beeswax
borax
box
boxer
boxing
coax
complex
convex
duplex
earwax
ex
exchange
exclaim
exclude
excuse
exercise
exit
expand
expect
expel
experience
expert
expire
expiry
explain
explained
explode

explore
express
extend
extendable
extensive
extent
extinct
extra
extreme
fax
fix
fixed
fixture
flex
flux
fox
foxtrot
galaxy
hexagon
hoax
icebox
index
jinx
larynx
latex
laxative
lynx
mailbox
max
maxi
maximum

mix
mixer
next
onyx
ox
oxide
oxygen
peroxide
perplex
pixie
pox
prefix
premix
reflex
reflux
relax
remix
saxophone
sex
sexist
six
sixteen
sixth
sixty
suffix
tax
taxi
taxing
text
textile
thorax

toxic
toxin
tuxedo
unbox
unisex
vex
wax
waxy

◆ **x**

(/e/ + /k/ +/s/)
x-ray

(/g/ +/zh/)
luxurious

(/k/ +/sh/)
luxury

◆ **xc**

exceed
excel
excellent
except
excess
excessive
excite
excited

◆ **xe**

annexe
axe
deluxe
pickaxe

MY NOTES

The yak yawned on the yellow yacht.
Yell yes to yummy yoghurt.

Graphemes

● **y**

backyard
barnyard
biyearly
churchyard
courtyard
farmyard
graveyard
lanyard
lightyear
schoolyard
scrapyard
yacht
yachtsman
yachtswoman
yak
yam
yank
yap
yard
yardage
yardstick
yarn
yarner
yarrow
yawn
yawned
yay
yeah
year
yearbook

yearling
yearly
yearn
yeast
yell
yelled
yellow
yellowed
yellowish
yellows
yells
yelp
yelped
yen
yep
yes
yesterday
yesteryear
yet
yeti
yield
yielded
yike
yikes
yip
yipes
yippee
yob
yobbery
yobbish
yodel

yodelled
yodeller
yoga
yoghurt
yogi
yoke
yolk
yolkless
yonder
yonks
yore
york
yorker
young
younger
youngster
your
yours
yourself
yow
yowl
yowls
yo-yo
yucca
yuck
yucky
yule
yum
yummy
yuppie
yurt

MY NOTES

The crazy wizard sneezed on the lazy lizard.
The noisy dogs ate the raspberry cookies in the desert.

Graphemes

🟡 **z**	ozone	🟡 **zz**	🟦 **s**	laser	wasn't	maize
ablaze	prize	abuzz	always	legs	Wednesday	ooze
amaze	quiz	blizzard	amusing	music		seize
blaze	realize	buzz	as	musical	🟦 **se**	sneeze
blazer	seized	buzzer	babies	news	because	snooze
breezy	size	dazzle	bananas	noisy	blouse	squeeze
citizen	sneezed	dizzy	bees	nose	browse	tweeze
cozy	unzip	drizzle	boys	nosy	bruise	wheeze
crazy	vaporize	fizz	busier	observation	cause	◆ **si**
ditzy	wheezy	fizzle	busily	observe	cheese	business
doze	wizard	fizzy	busy	poison	choose	◆ **ss**
dozen	zag	frizz	cars	poisonous	cruise	dessert
energize	zany	frizzy	chose	present	disease	dissolve
faze	zap	fuzz	confuse	raisin	ease	scissors
freezer	zapper	fuzzy	cookies	raspberry	erase	◆ x_1
froze	zebra	grizzly	cousin	reason	lose	anxiety
frozen	zed	guzzle	desert	refuse	noise	xylophone
gaze	zero	guzzler	dogs	rose	pause	◆ x_2
glaze	zest	jacuzzi	easily	roses	phase	(/g/+/z/)
glazed	zig	jazz	easy	season	phrase	exact
graze	zigzag	jazzy	eraser	stories	please	exactly
hazard	zillion	muzzle	flowers	toes	praise	exam
haze	zinc	nozzle	friends	toys	tease	examine
hazel	zing	nuzzle	fuse	treason		example
horizon	zip	puzzle	girls	trees	🟦 **ze**	exempt
kazoo	zipper	puzzled	has	Tuesday	analyze	exert
lazy	zits	quizzed	hers	unused	breeze	exhaust
lizard	zone	sizzle	his	use	bronze	exile
magazine	zoo	snazzy	is	visit	freeze	exist
maze	zoom	swizzle	keys	visitor	frieze	existence
oversize	zoos	whizz	knees	was	froze	
					gauze	

MY NOTES

The entourage will sabotage the camouflage.
Television causes occasional delusion.

Graphemes

◆ g
aubergine
courgette
genre
regime

◆ ge
barrage
beige
camouflage
collage
concierge
corsage
decoupage
dressage
entourage
massage
montage
rouge
sabotage

◆ s
casual
casually
casualty
closure
composure
enclosure
erasure
exposure
immeasurable
leisure
leisurely
measurable
measure
measurement
pleasurable
pleasure
remeasurement
treasure
treasury
unusual
usual
usually
visual
visualization
visually

◆ si
abrasion
amnesia
collision
conclusion
confusion
contusion
corrosion
decision
delusion
delusional
diffusion
disillusion
diversion
division
divisional
elusion
envision
erasion
erosion
exclusion
explosion
fusion
illusion
inclusion
infusion
intrusion
invasion
lesion
occasion
occasional
precision
provision
provisionally
revision
seclusion
television
version
vision
visionary

◆ ti
equation
equational

◆ z
azure
seizure

An Introduction to Phonics
Graphemes to Phonemes Word Bank
Copyright ©2024 Barrina J Mills

● Reception Class/New to English   ■ Year 1   ◆ Year 2 and above

a

/a/ ● pg15

apple	candle	gnat	ladder	nappy	ran
back	dragon	hammer	lamp	paddle	trap
badge	fan	hand	mad	pan	unhappy
bag	fang	handle	magic	quack	van
camp	flag	jam	man	ramp	wax

/ai/ ■ pg17

ache	April	cable	label	paper	stranger
acorn	apron	cradle	lady	stable	table
angel	baby	dangerous	nation	station	taste
apricot	bathe	famous	nature	strange	waste

/air/ ■ pg19

area	glaring	preparing	sharing	various	wariness
carer	parents	scary	staring	vary	wary

/ar/ ■ pg21

basket	class	drama	glasses	mask	plaster
bath	craft	fast	grass	pasture	pyjamas
branch	dance	flask	last	path	raspberry
castle	dancer	glass	lava	plant	unmask

/o/ ■ pg59

quad	squash	swan	wallet	was	watch
quality	swab	swap	wand	wash	what
quarrel	swallow	swat	wander	washer	whatever
squad	swamp	waffle	want	wasp	whatnot

/or/ ■ pg69

all	although	ball	halt	small	wall
almost	always	fall	salt	stall	water
alright	bald	hall	scald	tall	wrath

/uh/ ■ pg93

about	afraid	animal	banana	opera	special
above	allow	apply	capable	pedal	via
across	amaze	around	elephant	pizza	vitamin
address	amount	balloon	equal	several	woman

/e/ ◆ pg31

any	anyhow	anyone	anytime	anywhere	manyfold
anybody	anymore	anything	anyway	many	

/i/ ◆ pg45

bandage	damage	language	message	palace	sewage
blockage	forage	luggage	orange	plumage	storage
cabbage	image	manage	package	savage	surface

a-e

/ai/ ■ pg17

ate	cave	grave	name	safe	space
bake	female	lake	page	shake	tale
brave	flame	lane	place	shape	trace
cake	game	make	plate	skate	wake
came	grape	male	race	snake	wave

ach

/o/ ◆ pg59

yacht	yachtsman
yachting	yachtswoman

ae

/ai/ ◆ pg17

reggae
sundae

/air/ ◆ pg19

aerial	aeroplane	aerospace
aerobics	aerosol	

/ee/ ◆ pg35

algae
larvae

ah

/ar/ ◆ pg21

blah
hurrah

ai	/ai/ ●pg17	afraid	faint	mail	praise	snail	trail
		aim	gain	nail	rail	sprain	train
		brain	grain	pain	rain	stain	trainers
		chain	hail	paint	rainbow	strainer	waist
		drain	maid	painter	sail	tail	waiter
	/air/ ■pg19	airily	airing	dairy	fairish	fairyland	pairing
		airiness	airy	fairies	fairy	hairy	prairie
	/e/ ■pg31	again	said				
		against	unsaid				
	/i/ ◆pg45	fountain					
		mountain					

| aigh | /ai/ ◆pg17 | straight | straighter | | | | |
| | | straighten | | | | | |

air	/air/ ●pg19	airbag	airport	chair	hairball	hairpin	repair
		airborne	airspace	chairlift	hairbrush	highchair	stairs
		aircraft	airtight	downstairs	haircut	lair	stairway
		airflow	airway	funfair	hairless	pair	upstairs
		airmail	armchair	hair	hairnet	pushchair	wheelchair

| aire | /air/ ◆pg19 | billionaire | questionnaire | | | | |
| | | millionaire | trillionaire | | | | |

| ais | /igh/ ◆pg47 | aisle | | | | | |

al	/or/ ■pg69	beanstalk	sleepwalk	talk			
		chalk	stalk	walk			
	/ar/ ◆pg21	balm	calf	calming	half	palm	
		balmy	calm	calves	halves		

ar	/ar/ ●pg21	alarm	barber	carpet	garden	jar	scarf
		argue	bark	cartwheel	garlic	marble	shark
		ark	barn	dark	hard	parcel	smart
		arm	car	farmer	harp	park	sparkle
		artist	cardigan	farmyard	harvest	party	star
	/air/ ◆pg19	scarce	scarcity				
		scarcely					
	/or/ ◆pg69	award	quarter	swarm	wardrobe	warm	warn
		dwarf	reward	war	wards	warmth	warp
	/uh/ ◆pg93	collar	pillar	similar	sugar		
		leopard	popular	solar	vinegar		

are	/air/ ■pg19	aftercare	barely	childcare	fanfare	hare	rarely
		airfare	beware	compares	fare	mare	scare
		aware	care	cookware	flares	nightmare	share
		bare	careful	dare	glare	prepare	snare
		barefoot	careless	declare	hardware	rare	spare

au	/or/ ■pg69	applause	aura	autumn	faulty	laundry	sauna
		astronaut	author	cause	haunt	pause	taunt
		August	auto	fault	launch	sauce	taut
	/ar/ ◆pg21	aunt	draught	laugh	laughing		
		aunty	draughty	laughable	laughter		
	/o/ ◆pg59	because					
		sausage					
	/oa/ ◆pg61	chauffeur					
		mauve					

augh	/or/ ■pg69	caught	taught				
		daughter					
		naughty					

| aur | /or/ ◆pg69 | dinosaur | | | | | |

aw	/or/ ■pg69	awful	crawl	flaw	paw	sawn	thaw
		awkward	dawdle	gnaw	prawn	shawl	trawl
		awning	dawn	hawk	raw	spawn	trawler
		brawl	draw	jaw	saw	sprawl	withdraw
		claw	fawn	law	sawdust	straw	yawn

ay	/ai/ ■pg17	always	day	lay	playful	slay	today
		array	decay	okay	pray	spray	tray
		away	delay	pay	railway	stay	way
		clay	display	play	ray	stray	x-ray
		crayon	fray	players	relay	sway	yesterday
	/ee/ ◆pg35	quay					

b	/b/ ●pg23	airbag	big	boot	brush	buzz	robin
		baby	bike	brain	bucket	celebrate	table
		badge	bin	brave	bug	crab	tube
		bag	bird	bread	bus	cub	web
		bib	book	broom	bush	herb	zebra

bb	/b/ ●pg23	bobbin	dabble	hobby	rabbit	scabby	squabble
		bobbles	dribble	jabbed	ribbon	scrabble	stubble
		bubble	ebbed	knobbly	robber	scribble	tabby
		cabbage	grabbed	nibble	rubbish	shabby	webbed
		cobbler	grubby	pebbles	rubble	slobber	wobble

bt	/t/ ◆pg83	debt	redoubt				
		doubt	subtle				
		misdoubt					

c	/k/ ●pg25	acorn	calf	car	conker	crawl	cup
		cab	camera	clap	cook	crayon	curly
		cactus	candle	cloud	cooker	cross	custard
		cage	cap	coat	cow	crow	electric
		cake	cape	coin	crab	crowd	picnic
	/s/ ■pg79	accent	ceiling	centimetre	city	medicine	saucy
		accept	celery	centipede	cycle	pencil	specific
		access	cell	cinema	dancer	princess	spicy
		bicycle	cement	circus	December	recipe	vaccinate
	/ch/ ◆pg27	cellist					
		cello					

cc	/k/ ◆pg25	hiccup	occur				
		occasion	soccer				
		occupy					

ce	/s/ ■pg79	chance	juice	palace	police	prince	silence
		dance	justice	peace	pounce	sauce	since
		fence	lettuce	pence	practice	saucepan	space
		glance	office	piece	prance	sentence	voice
	/sh/ ◆pg81	liquorice					
		ocean					

ch

/ch/ ●pg27

arch	brooch	champ	child	highchair	rich
beach	bunch	cheek	chimney	inch	search
belch	chain	cheerful	chin	lunch	teach
bench	chair	chick	chip	pouch	teacher
branch	chalk	chicken	crunchy	punch	torch

/j/ ◆pg49

- ostrich
- sandwich
- spinach

/k/ ◆pg25

aching	chemist	chord	echo	psychic	school
chaos	choir	chorus	orchid	scheme	stomach

/sh/ ◆pg81

chandelier	machine
chef	parachute
chute	

che

/k/ ◆pg25

ache	heartache
headache	toothache

/sh/ ◆pg81

cache	niche
crèche	quiche
moustache	

ci

/sh/ ◆pg81

artificial	especially	gracious	official	precious	special
delicious	facial	musician	optician	social	vicious

ck

/k/ ●pg25

back	chicken	kick	pickle	snack	ticket
black	clock	lick	quack	socks	track
block	crack	lock	rock	stick	trick
brick	duckling	luck	sack	sticker	truck
buckle	gecko	neck	sick	suck	yuck

cqu

/k/ ◆pg25

- lacquer
- racquet

/k/+/w/ ◆pg75

acquaint	acquirable	acquiree
acquaintance	acquire	acquit
acquainted	acquired	acquitted

d

/d/ ●pg29

adult	bird	deep	friend	loud	sad
bandage	blood	deer	goodbye	mend	slide
bed	body	den	ground	pod	stand
bedroom	bud	desk	hand	pond	toad
bend	building	field	handle	red	wand

/j/ ◆pg49

educate	procedure
graduate	soldier
graduation	
individual	

dd

/d/ ●pg29

add	caddy	kidding	nodded	pudding	shredding
address	cuddle	ladder	odd	puddle	skidding
bedding	haddock	middle	paddle	redden	teddy
bladder	hidden	muddle	paddling	sadden	toddler
buddies	huddle	muddy	peddle	saddle	udder

dge

/j/ ■pg49

abridge	dredge	fudge	knowledge	pledge	smidge
badge	drudge	grudge	ledge	porridge	smudge
bridge	edge	hedge	lodge	ridge	stodge
budge	fledge	hedgehog	midge	sledge	trudge
dodge	fridge	judge	nudge	sludge	wedge

dj

/j/ ◆pg49

adjacent	adjourn
adjective	adjust
adjoin	

e

/e/ pg31	bed	correct	egg	letter	pet	tennis
	bell	den	empty	net	red	vet
	belt	dentist	hen	pen	shell	wet
	bend	dress	jet	pencil	smell	yellow
	bent	edge	leg	pepper	ten	yes
/ee/ pg35	be	emu	even	he	neon	she
	demon	equal	female	me	scenic	we
/uh/ pg93	celebrate	open	seven	the		
	enemy	operate	shaken	towel		
	fire	problem	taken	wire		
/ear/ pg33	era					
/i/ pg45	banquet	believe	beside	elephant	erratic	prevent
	begin	beloved	between	enormous	event	record
	behave	below	effect	epiphany	present	television
	behind	beneath	effective	erase	pretty	women

e-e

/ee/ pg35	athlete	concrete	evening	obese	recede	theme
	compete	delete	extreme	obsolete	scene	these
	complete	eve	extremely	precede	swede	trapeze

ea

/ai/ pg17	break	daybreak	greatest			
	breaking	great	steak			
	breakup	greater				
/e/ pg31	bread	dreamt	healthy	leather	sweat	tread
	breakfast	feather	heaven	meadow	sweater	treasure
	dead	head	heavy	measure	sweaty	unhealthy
	deaf	headset	jealous	spread	thread	weather
/ee/ pg35	beach	breathe	leak	peanut	seal	stream
	bead	dream	leap	peas	seat	tea
	beak	easel	meal	please	speak	teacher
	bean	eat	peace	read	squeak	treat
	beast	leaf	peach	sea	steal	wheat
/ear/ pg33	appearing	dearest	idea	nearing	smearing	wearily
	clearing	hearing	nearest	shearing	teary	weary

ear

/ear/ pg33	appeared	dear	earlobe	fearless	rear	tearful
	beard	ear	earring	hear	sheared	tears
	clear	eardrum	fear	nearby	smear	year
/air/ pg19	bear	footwear	neckwear	overbear	sportswear	tear
	eyewear	knitwear	nightwear	pear	swear	wear
/ar/ pg21	heart	heartily	hearty			
	hearth	heartless				
/er/ pg37	earl	earth	hearse	pearl	researcher	unheard
	early	earthling	learn	rehearse	search	unlearn
	earn	heard	overheard	research	unearth	yearns

eau

/oa/ pg61	bureau					
	gateau					
	plateau					
/ue/ pg91	beaut	beautifully				
	beautician	beautify				
	beautiful	beauty				

ed

/d/ pg29	banged	claimed	darkened	joined	prayed	stayed
	banned	cleared	drained	opened	rolled	strayed
	begged	crawled	frayed	played	sprayed	turned
/d/ pg29	craved	dyed	lived	moved	raised	tied
	damaged	grazed	loved	praised	saved	used

ed							
	/i/+/d/ ■pg29 & 45	addicted boarded bonded	crowded deleted granted	landed lifted noted	parted planted pounded	recorded rested started	wanted winded
	/t/ ■pg 83	backed blessed blocked brushed chipped	coughed cracked cramped crushed dipped	dropped finished fixed hooked jumped	kicked laughed linked marched marked	mixed parked peaked puffed ripped	sacked stacked talked tapped touched

ee							
	/ee/ ●pg35	asleep bee beef cheek cheese	eel feet fifteen geese green	heel knee kneecap peel queen	see seed sheep sleep sleet	sleeve street sweep sweet teeth	three tree weed week wheelchair
	/ear/ ◆pg33	cheering domineering	eerie eerily	engineering jeering	steering veering		

eer						
	/ear/ ■pg33	auctioneer beer career cheer	cheerful deer domineer engineer	jeer leer peer pioneer	puppeteer queer reindeer sheer	sneer steer veer volunteer

ei				
	/ai/ ◆pg17	beige reiki	reindeer veil	vein
	/e/ ◆pg31	heifer leisure	leisurely	
	/ear/ ◆pg33	madeira		
	/ee/ ◆pg35	ceiling deceive	receipt receive	seize seizure
	/igh/ ◆pg47	eider eiderdown	either neither	

eigh							
	/ai/ ■pg17	eight eighteen	eighth flyweight	freight neigh	neighbour outweigh	sleigh weigh	weight weightless
	/igh/ ◆pg47	height heighten	sleight				

eir			
	/air/ ◆pg19	their theirs	
	/ear/ ◆pg33	weird weirdest	weirdly weirdo

eo			
	/e/ ◆pg31	jeopardize jeopardy	leopard
	/ee/ ◆pg35	people	

er							
	/er/ ●pg37	concern dessert expert fern gerbil	germ her herbal herd kerb	merge mermaid merman nervous observe	perch perfect perm person preserve	reserved reverse serve swerve term	thermal universe university verbal vertical
	/uh/ ●pg93	after baker better bitter brother	corner cover dancer dinner farmer	father flower hamster letter litter	mister monster mother paper plaster	power printer river silver sister	sticker summer teacher under winter

ere						
/air/ ■pg19	anywhere	elsewhere	nowhere	somewhere	thereafter	therefore
	compere	everywhere	premiere	there	thereby	where
/er/ ■pg37	were					
/ear/ ◆pg33	adhere	hereby	severe	sincere	sphere	
	here	interfere	severely	sincerely	werewolf	

et				
/ai/ ◆pg17	ballet	buffet	croquet	sachet
	bouquet	crochet	gourmet	sorbet

eu					
/ue/ ◆pg91	eucalyptus	feud	neutral	neutron	pneumonia
	euphemism	feudal	neutralize	pneumatic	pseudonym

ew						
I /oo/ ■pg65	blew	chew	drew	grew	sewage	unscrew
	brew	crew	flew	screw	threw	withdrew
/ue/ ■pg91	curfew	fewer	nephew	news	renew	spew
	dew	knew	new	newt	skew	stew
	few	mildew	newbie	phew	skewer	stewing
/oa/ ◆pg61	sew					
	sewn					

ey					
/ee/ 1 ■pg35	key	off-key			
	ley				
/ee/ 2 ■pg35	alley	donkey	money	ropey	valley
	chimney	journey	monkey	turkey	
/ai/ ◆pg17	drey	obey	survey		
	grey	prey	they		

eye			
/igh/ ■pg47	eye	eyelash	eyelid
	eyebrow	eyelet	eyesight

f						
/f/ ●pg39	beef	fan	fifteen	flower	four	fun
	deaf	farm	fish	fog	fox	golf
	fairy	fart	fix	food	frog	lift
	fall	feet	flag	fork	fruit	wolf
/v/ ■pg95	of	whereof				
	thereof					

ff						
/f/ ●pg39	afford	coffin	effort	muffin	puffer	stuff
	buffet	cuff	fluff	off	raffle	stuffy
	cliff	different	fluffy	officer	scruffy	toffee
	coffee	effect	giraffe	puff	sniff	waffle

g						
/g/ ●pg41	alligator	burger	finger	gap	girl	pig
	argue	clog	flag	garden	give	stag
	bag	dig	fog	gate	grape	tangle
	big	dog	frog	gaze	grass	twig
	bug	dragon	game	gift	grow	wig
/j/ ■pg49	badger	dangerous	gel	germ	giraffe	page
	cage	detergent	gem	giant	gym	stage
	danger	engine	gerbil	ginger	magic	stranger
/zh/ ◆pg105	aubergine	genre				
	courgette	regime				

ge						
/j/ ■pg49	bandage	cottage	hinge	manage	revenge	surge
	binge	courage	huge	orange	sewage	surgeon
	blockage	damage	language	package	singe	urge
	cabbage	forage	large	plumage	storage	village
	change	fringe	luggage	range	strange	voyage

ge	/zh/ ◆pg105	barrage beige	camouflage collage	concierge corsage	decoupage dressage	entourage massage	montage sabotage
gg	/g/ ●pg41	baggage baggy begged buggy dagger	digger egg eggcup foggy giggle	goggle haggle jiggle jogging juggler	luggage maggot muggy nugget pegged	saggy shaggy snuggle soggy struggle	tagged toggle twiggy wiggle wriggly
	/j/ ◆pg49	exaggerate suggest	veggie				
gh	/f/ ◆pg39	cough enough	laugh laughter	rough tough	trough		
	/g/ ◆pg41	aghast ghastly	gherkin ghost	ghosting			
gm	/m/ ◆pg53	diaphragm paradigm	phlegm				
gn	/n/ ◆pg55	align alignment assign benign	campaign design feign foreign	foreigner gnarl gnarly gnash	gnat gnaw gnome gnomic	gnomish gnosis gnu malign	realign reign resign sign
gu	/g/ ◆pg41	guarantee guess	guests guidance	guide guidebook	guilt guilty	guise guitar	
gue	/g/ ◆pg41	catalogue colleague	dialogue fatigue	intrigue league	morgue plague	prologue rogue	vague vogue
h	/h/ ●pg43	greenhouse hairbrush hairy half hall	hamburger hammer hammock hamper hamster	hand handle hanger happy harvest	hat hello help hippo hole	home honey hood hook hoop	hop hug hum hungry hurdle
hei	/air/ ◆pg19	heiress					
heir	/air/ ◆pg19	heir heirdom	heirloom heirship				
ho	/ou/ ◆pg71	hour hourly					
i	/i/ ●pg45	big bin blink bridge children	chilly dinner dish drink finger	hill holiday igloo ink insect	knit mitt pin pink prince	princess quick ring ship shrink	sick sing sink six skin
	/uh/ ■pg93	April family	incredible invisible	pencil stencil			
	/a/ ◆pg15	meringue					
	/ee/ ◆pg35	antique boutique	machine mosquito	physique police	quiche quinoa	sardine	
	/igh/ ◆pg47	behind blind child find	grind hindsight idea ideal	identify identity kind library	mild mind private remind	science sizes spider tidy	title wild wind writer

Grapheme	Sound / page					
i-e	/igh/ ■pg47	beside	five	like	pipe	ripe	time
		bike	hide	mice	polite	shine	white
		bite	ice	nine	prize	smile	wide
		dive	invite	outside	rice	stripe	wipe
		drive	knife	pile	ride	surprise	write
ie	/igh/ ■pg47	classifies	die	flies	lies	specifies	ties
		complies	died	fried	outflies	spied	tried
		cried	dies	fries	pie	spies	tries
		cries	dried	implies	replies	supplies	untie
		denies	dries	lie	skies	tie	
	/e/ ◆pg31	befriend	friend	unfriendly			
		boyfriend	girlfriend				
	/ee/ ◆pg35	believe	chief	grief	piece	relief	shriek
		brief	field	niece	priest	shield	thief
	/i/ ◆pg45	sieve					
ier	/ear/ ◆pg33	cashier	frontier	piercing			
		fierce	pier	tier			
		fiercely	pierce	tierce			
iew	/ue/ ◆pg91	interview	preview	view	viewer	viewless	
		overview	review	viewable	viewfinder	viewpoint	
igh	/igh/ ●pg47	airtight	flight	highest	lighter	right	thigh
		bright	fright	highlight	midnight	sigh	tight
		daylight	frighten	knight	night	sight	tighten
		delightful	high	light	nightfall	slight	tonight
		fight	highchair	lightening	nightlife	spotlight	upright
ir	/er/ ■pg37	affirm	circle	dirty	quirky	stir	thirteen
		birch	circuit	fir	shirt	swirl	thirteenth
		bird	circular	firm	sir	third	thirty
		birth	circus	first	skirt	thirst	twirl
		chirp	dirt	girl	smirk	thirsty	whirl
	/igh/ ◆pg47	fire	fireside	wire			
		firefly	iron	wireless			
is	/igh/ ◆pg47	island	isle				
		islander					
j	/j/ ●pg49	ajar	jam	jelly	job	journal	jump
		enjoy	jar	jet	jog	judo	jumper
		injection	jaw	jewellery	join	jug	jungle
		jacket	jazz	jiggle	joke	juggle	junk
		jail	jeep	jingle	jolly	juice	subject
k	/k/ ●pg25	ankle	break	king	oink	skate	stalk
		bark	dark	kiss	park	skin	talk
		beak	fork	kitten	pink	skip	thank
		blink	ink	market	sank	skirt	wink
		book	key	milk	sink	speak	work
kk	/k/ ◆pg25	trekked					
		trekking					
kn	/n/ ■pg55	knack	knee	knew	knives	knoll	known
		knackered	kneecap	knife	knob	knot	knows
		knave	kneel	knight	knobbly	know	knuckle
		knead	knelt	knit	knock	knowledge	unknown

Grapheme	Phoneme						
l	/l/ ●pg51	black	curl	lace	leg	loud	melon
		blood	flask	lamb	lick	love	owl
		blow	flood	lap	lid	lower	pool
		clock	flower	laugh	light	luck	quilt
		crawl	label	learn	lock	mail	slap
le	/l/ ■pg51	aisle	hairstyle	restyle			
		freestyle	isle	style			
		gargoyle	lifestyle	voile			
	/uh/ then /l/ ■pg51 & 93	ankle	buckle	goggle	middle	pickle	single
		apple	candle	juggle	needle	puddle	stable
		bicycle	circle	jungle	noodle	purple	table
		bubble	giggle	kettle	pebble	puzzle	tickle
ll	/l/ ●pg51	ball	bull	football	lollipop	quill	telly
		balloon	collar	grill	lolly	roller	trolley
		bell	doll	hello	pill	silly	wall
		belly	drill	hill	pillar	small	yell
		brolly	follow	jelly	pillow	swallow	yellow
m	/m/ ●pg53	alarm	dream	magic	mess	mop	stream
		animal	farm	map	milk	mouse	sum
		bottom	ham	mat	mirror	mug	swim
		broom	hem	mermaid	money	room	tram
		cream	jam	merman	moon	storm	warm
mb	/m/ ◆pg53	bomb	crumb	lamb	outclimb	succumb	upclimb
		climb	dumb	limb	plumb	thumb	womb
		comb	honeycomb	numb	plumber	tomb	
me	/m/ ■pg53	awesome	enzyme	handsome	loathsome	overcome	tiresome
		become	fearsome	income	lonesome	regime	welcome
		come	gruesome	irksome	outcome	some	wholesome
mm	/m/ ●pg53	ammonia	dimmed	hammer	mammal	scammer	summer
		comment	drummer	hammock	mammoth	shimmer	summon
		commit	dummy	hummed	mummify	simmer	swimmer
		common	gammon	immerge	plummet	skimmed	tummy
		dilemma	grammar	immune	rummage	summary	yummy
mn	/m/ ◆pg53	autumn	condemn	hymn	solemn		
		column	damn	limn			
n	/n/ ●pg55	ant	garden	night	pant	run	town
		burn	green	nine	pen	snail	train
		coin	human	nod	queen	snow	unicorn
		corn	moon	nose	rain	spin	won
		den	nap	paint	reindeer	ten	yawn
	/ng/ ◆pg57	angle	anxious	conker	hungry	oink	sink
		angler	bank	donkey	ink	pink	skunk
		angry	blanket	drink	jungle	prank	tango
		ankle	blink	finger	junk	rink	twinkle
		anxiety	bunk	hunger	mango	shrink	wrinkle
ng	/ng/ ●pg57	bang	evening	morning	ring	sting	tong
		biting	gong	nothing	sing	string	wedding
		building	hanger	outing	singer	strong	wing
		cling	icing	pudding	sling	stung	wrong
		duckling	long	recycling	song	swing	young

ngue	/ng/ ◆pg57	meringue tongue tongueless					

nn	/n/ ●pg55	annoy annual banner beginner bonnet	bunny cannot dinner fennel flannel	funnel funny henna inner kennel	manners penny pinned planner punnet	runner runny scanned spinner sunny	swanning tenner tennis tunnel winner

o							
	/o/ ●pg59	block body bottle box chop	clock dog dot flock fog	fox frock frog hop jog	knock knot lock long mop	off on pocket pop rocket	shop socks soft spot stop
	/oa/ ■pg61	cargo cold comb domino	echo fold gold golden	hello hotel mobile moped	ocean old older open	over photo poem poet	radio sofa total yo-yo
	l /oo/ ■pg65	do disprove	improve lose	move movie	prove remove	tomb who	whom womb
	/or/ ■pg69	boring snoring storage	story storyteller				
	/u/ ■pg89	above colour colourful compass	cover dove dozen front	glove honey love money	monkey month mother onion	oven shove shovel son	ton undone won worry
	/uh/ ■pg93	bottom dinosaur	dozen history	nation occur	other parrot	ration today	tomorrow tonight
	/w/+/u/ ■pg97	once one oneness	oneself onesie				
	/i/ ◆pg45	women					
	s /oo/ ◆pg67	werewolf wolf wolfish	woman womanhood womanly				
	/ou/ ◆pg71	flour our ourself	scour sour				

o-e	/oa/ ■pg61	alone bone broke choke close	cone drove froze globe hole	home hose joke lobe mole	nose phone poke rope rose	slope smoke spoke stone telephone	throne vote whole woke wrote

oa	/oa/ ●pg61	boast boat bloat cloak coach	coast coat croak float foal	foam goal goalie goat groan	load loaf moan oak oats	poach road roast shoal soak	soap throat toad toast toaster
	/or/ ◆pg69	abroad broad broaden					

oar	/or/ ◆pg69	aboard boar	boarding boards	coarse hoard	hoarder hoarse	oars roar	soar uproar

oe	/ee/ ◆pg35	coeliac diarrhoea	phoenix				
	/oa/ ◆pg61	aloe cargoes dingoes	doe dominoes echoes	foe forgoes goes	hoe oboe roe	sloe tiptoe toe	toenail woe woeful
	l /oo/ ◆pg65	canoe canoeing	shoe shoebox	shoehorn shoelace	shoestring shoetree		
	/u/ ◆pg89	does doesn't					

| oi | /oi/ ●pg63 | appoint
avoid
boil
choice
coil | coiling
coin
foil
hoist
join | joiner
joint
jointly
joist
koi | moisture
noise
noisy
oil
oink | ointment
pinpoint
point
poison
soil | soiled
spoil
toilet
uncoil
voice |

oo	l /oo/ ●pg65	balloon bathroom boot broom cartoon	drool droop hoop hooves igloo	kangaroo moo moon noodle poo	pool roof room root school	scooter shampoo smooth snooze spoon	stool tool tooth zoo zoom
	s /oo/ ●pg67	book bookcase booklet cook	cooker cookies fishhook foot	football footless good goodbye	hood hoodie looking oops	shook stood wood wooden	woodpecker woof wool woolly
	/u/ ■pg89	blood flood					
	/oa/ ◆pg61	brooch brooches					

| oor | /or/ ■pg69 | door
doorway | floor
poor | poorly | | | |

or	/or/ ●pg69	adorn afford born cord cork	corn for fork form fort	forty horn horse lord morning	orb order porch pork scorch	short snorkel sport stork storm	sword thorn torch torn worn
	/er/ ■pg37	artwork legwork network	word wordy work	worker workman workout	world worldly worm	wormery worse worship	worst worth worthy
	/uh/ ◆pg93	actor alligator	doctor minor	motor scissors	visitor		

| ore | /or/ ◆pg69 | ashore
before
bore | core
explore
more | ore
pore
score | shore
snore
store | swore
tore
wore | |

ou	/ou/ ●pg71	blouse bounce bouncy cloud cloudy	couch count counter found fountain	ground hound house loud mountain	mouse mouth ouch out outdoor	pouch pout proud round shout	sound south sprout thousand trousers
	/o/ ◆pg59	cough coughed	coughing trough				
	/oa/ ◆pg61	bouquet mould	poultry shoulder	soul soulful			
	l /oo/ ◆pg65	group route	router soup	wound wounded			

Grapheme	Sound					
ou	/u/ ◆pg89	country couple	cousin double	enormous enough	nourish rough	touch tough	trouble young
	/uh/ ◆pg93	curious famous	joyous vicious	vigorous			
ough	/oa/ ◆pg61	although dough	doughnut furlough	though			
	l /oo/ ◆pg65	through throughout					
	/or/ ◆pg69	bought brought	fought nought	ought sought	thought wrought		
	/ou/ ◆pg71	bough drought	plough slough				
	/uh/ ◆pg93	borough thorough					
oul	s /oo/ ◆pg67	could could've couldn't couldn't've	should should've shouldn't shouldn't've	would would've wouldn't wouldn't've			
our	/er/ ◆pg37	adjourn journal	journey				
	/or/ ◆pg69	course court	courtyard four	fourth mourn	pour sourced	your yourself	
	/uh/ ◆pg93	armour colour	favour flavour	neighbour odour	rigour rumour	savour vigour	
ow	/oa/ ■pg61	arrow blow borrow bow bowl	crow elbow flow flown follow	grow grown know known low	meadow mow narrow own owner	pillow rainbow shadow shallow slow	snow sow throw window yellow
	/ou/ ■pg71	bow brow brown brownie clown	cow crowd crown down downhill	downside drown drowsy flower frown	growl how howl meow owl	powder powerful prowl scowl shower	towel tower town vowel wow
oy	/oi/ ■pg63	ahoy alloy annoy boy buoy	corduroy cowboy coy decoy destroy	employ employer enjoy enjoyment envoy	foyer joy joyful joyfully loyal	loyally loyalty overjoy oyster royal	soybean tomboy toy toyshop voyage
p	/p/ ●pg73	cap cup drop gap hip	jump lamp limp nap open	pair park pea pen pet	pick pig pink play pool	pot proud pull purple put	ripe sip sleep slip zip
ph	/f/ ■pg39	alpha alphabet aphids autograph dolphin	elephant epiphany graph grapheme morph	nephew nymph paragraph phantom phase	phew phobia phone phoneme phonics	phony photo photocopy photograph phrase	physical saxophone sphere telephone trophy
pn	/n/ ◆pg55	pneuma pneumatic	pneumonia pneumonic				

pp	/p/ • pg73	appear	dropped	hippo	popped	ripped	tapping
		apple	flappy	kipper	popper	ripple	topping
		clapping	floppy	nappy	poppy	slipper	upper
		cropped	happily	nippy	puppet	supper	wrapper
		cuppa	happy	pepper	puppy	swapped	zipper

| **ps** | /s/ ◆pg79 | psych | psycho | | | | |
| | | psychic | psychology | | | | |

| **pt** | /t/ ◆pg83 | nonreceipt | | | | | |
| | | receipt | | | | | |

qu	/k/+/w/ • pg75	aqua	earthquake	quarrel	quick	square	squid
		aquarium	liquid	quarter	quiet	squash	squirrel
		aquatic	quack	queen	quilt	squeak	tranquil
		banquet	quad	question	sequin	squeeze	turquoise
	/k/ ◆pg25	bouquet	croquet	marquee	quay	quinoa	
		conquer	lacquer	mosquito	quiche	tequila	

| **que** | /k/ ◆pg25 | antique | cheque | mosque | physique | plaque | technique |
| | | boutique | grotesque | opaque | pique | queue | unique |

r	/r/ • pg77	brick	drill	rabbit	red	roast	throat
		brown	drum	race	ribbon	rock	train
		crack	fairy	rag	ring	rope	trainer
		cricket	forest	rain	river	rose	tray
		cry	green	rainbow	road	run	tree

| **rh** | /r/ ◆pg77 | rhapsody | rheumatic | rhinoceros | rhubarb | rhyming | rhythmic |
| | | rhetoric | rhinestone | rhomboid | rhyme | rhythm | rhythmist |

rr	/r/ • pg77	arrive	borrow	curry	lorry	quarry	starry
		arrow	burrow	ferry	mirror	raspberry	strawberry
		barrel	carrot	furry	narrow	sorry	surround
		barrier	carry	horrid	parrot	sparrow	warrior
		berry	cherry	hurry	porridge	squirrel	worry

s	/s/ • pg79	bus	sail	sing	soap	sport	stone
		desk	sand	sink	soil	spy	sweet
		forest	seat	sit	song	stand	taste
		insect	see	sleep	soup	star	vest
		sack	sick	slide	spoon	stir	wasp
	/z/ ■pg103	amusing	cars	easy	his	noisy	rose
		as	chose	fuse	is	nose	toys
		bees	cousin	girls	laser	observe	use
		boys	desert	has	music	poison	visit
		busy	dogs	hers	news	present	was
	/sh/ ◆pg81	insurance	sure				
		sugar	surely				
	/zh/ ◆pg105	casual	closure	enclosure	leisure	pleasure	usual
		casualty	composure	exposure	measure	treasure	visual

| **sc** | /s/ ◆pg79 | fascinate | scenario | scenery | scent | science | |
| | | muscle | scene | scenic | scented | scissors | |

se	/s/ ■pg79	cease	decease	horse	loose	purse	rinse
		course	else	house	mouse	release	
	/z/ ■pg103	because	bruise	choose	ease	noise	please
		blouse	cause	cruise	erase	pause	praise
		browse	cheese	disease	lose	phrase	tease

sh	/sh/ ●pg81	brush	dish	rash	sheep	shop	shush
		bush	fish	rush	shell	short	shut
		cash	fresh	shade	ship	shout	splash
		cashew	mushroom	shape	shirt	show	wash
		cushion	posh	shark	shoe	shower	wish

si	/sh/ ◆pg81	conversion	expansion	mansion	tension		
		dimension	extension	pension			
	/z/ ◆pg103	business					
	/zh/ ◆pg105	abrasion	corrosion	division	illusion	occasion	seclusion
		amnesia	decision	envision	inclusion	precision	television
		collision	delusion	erosion	infusion	provision	version
		confusion	diversion	fusion	invasion	revision	visionary

ss	/s/ ●pg79	across	brass	fossil	hiss	mess	press
		address	dress	fuss	kiss	miss	sass
		boss	essence	grass	less	pass	
	/sh/ ◆pg81	assurance	reassure				
		assure	tissue				
		pressure					
	/z/ ◆pg103	dessert					
		dissolve					
		scissors					

| **ssi** | /sh/ ◆pg81 | compression | mission | permission | | | |
| | | discussion | passion | | | | |

| **st** | /s/ ■pg79 | castle | glisten | listen | thistle | | |
| | | fasten | jostle | listening | whistle | | |

| **sw** | /s/ ◆pg79 | answer | swordfish | | | | |
| | | sword | | | | | |

t	/t/ ●pg83	ant	feet	mat	potato	teeth	toy
		bite	foot	net	shut	ten	tray
		cat	gift	out	sit	test	tree
		cot	goat	paint	snot	time	vet
		dot	hat	pot	table	toilet	wet
	/ch/ ◆pg27	actual	capture	fortune	natural	nature	unnatural
		adventure	factual	misfortune	naturally	picture	venture

tch	/ch/ ◆pg27	batch	fetch	kitchen	pitch	sketch	swatch
		butcher	hatch	latch	pitcher	snatch	switch
		catch	itchy	matchstick	satchel	stitch	watch
		crutch	ketchup	patch	scratch	stretch	witch

| **te** | /t/ ■pg83 | baste | distaste | paste | route | taste | |
| | | caste | haste | reroute | suite | waste | |

th	v /th/ ●pg85	clothing	slither	than	then	this	whether
		feather	smooth	that	there	those	with
		lather	soothing	the	these	together	within
		other	teething	them	they	weather	without
	uv /th/ ●pg87	athlete	breath	health	teeth	throat	thunder
		author	earth	length	thank	thorn	toothbrush
		bath	fifth	month	thirsty	throw	truth
		birthday	forth	moth	three	thumb	warmth
	/t/ ◆pg83	thyme					

| the | v /th/ ■pg85 | bathe | clothe | loathe | seethe | sunbathe | unclothe |
| | | breathe | lathe | scathe | soothe | teethe | |

ti	/sh/ ◆pg81	addition	dedication	emotion	junction	petition	sedation
		affection	deletion	fiction	lotion	portion	station
		ambition	direction	fraction	mention	rotation	stationary
		caution	edition	intention	option	section	stationery
	/zh/ ◆pg105	equation					
		equational					

tt	/t/ ●pg83	better	bottom	gutter	natter	pitta	rattle
		bitten	butter	kettle	nettle	potty	settee
		bitter	button	kitten	nutty	pretty	sitting
		bottle	grotto	mitten	pattern	putty	splatter

u	/u/ ●pg89	blush	club	fun	jumper	munch	truck
		brush	cup	gum	lump	number	tusk
		bus	cut	hungry	lunch	run	umbrella
		button	drum	jug	mud	shut	up
		buzz	duck	jump	mug	sunny	uphill
	s /oo/ ■pg67	bull	bush	cushion	pudding	push	put
		bullion	bushy	full	pull	pushchair	sugar
		bully	butcher	output	pulley	pushy	sugary
	/ue/ ■pg91	dual	future	musical	stupid	unique	universe
		duality	human	musician	unicorn	unit	university
		duel	humanity	pupil	uniform	unite	unusual
		duo	menu	reunited	unify	united	usual
		duty	music	student	union	universal	usually
	/e/ ◆pg31	burial	bury				
		buried					
	/i/ ◆pg45	busier	busy				
		business					
	l /oo/ ◆pg65	plumage	ruler	truly	truthful		
		ruin	ruling	truth	unruly		
	/uh/ (1) ◆pg93	awful	fearful	helpful	lawful	tearful	
		beautiful	grateful	hopeful	mindful	thankful	
		careful	hateful	joyful	playful	useful	
	/uh/ (2) ◆pg93	focus	supply				
		supplier					
	/w/ ◆pg97	language					
		penguin					

u-e	l /oo/ ■pg65	absolute	elude	flume	June	rude	
		brute	exclude	flute	parachute	rule	
		chute	fluke	include	prune	salute	
	/ue/ ■pg91	amuse	consume	excuse	misuse	produce	tube
		amusement	costume	fume	mule	reduce	tune
		assume	cube	fuse	mute	refuse	use
		bemuse	cute	huge	nude	reproduce	useful
		confuse	duke	introduce	perfume	reuse	volume

ue	/ue/ ●pg91	argue	cue	miscue	rescue	tissue	virtue
		autocue	due	muesli	residue	Tuesday	
		avenue	endue	overdue	revenue	undue	
		barbecue	hue	pursue	statue	value	
		continue	issue	queue	subdue	venue	
	l /oo/ ■pg65	blue	cruel	sue			
		clue	glue	true			

ui	/i/ ◆pg45	biscuit	building				
		build	built				
		builder	circuit				
	I /oo/ ◆pg65	bruise	fruitful	suit			
		cruise	fruity	suitable			
		fruit	juice	unsuitable			

ur	/er/ ■pg37	burger	church	curly	gurgle	purse	turkey
		burglar	churn	cursive	hurdle	slurp	turn
		burn	curb	curtain	nurse	surf	turnip
		burp	curl	curve	nursery	turban	turtle
		burst	curling	furniture	purple	turf	yurt
	/uh/ ◆pg93	flour	our	Saturday	sour	survive	
		hour	ourself	scour	surprise		

ure	/uh/ ◆pg93	adventure	closure	future	injure	measure	picture
		capture	figure	gesture	lecture	nature	pleasure
	/oo/+/uh/ ◆pg93	immature					
		mature					
	/y/+/oo/ + /uh/ ◆pg93	cure	pure				
		insecure	secure				
		obscure					

| **uu** | /ue/ ◆pg91 | vacuum | | | | | |
| | | vacuumed | | | | | |

| **uy** | /igh/ ◆pg47 | buy | guy | | | | |
| | | buyer | | | | | |

v	/v/ ●pg95	brave	drive	hive	pave	van	vet
		caravan	evening	knives	river	vanish	violin
		cave	five	movie	seven	vein	voice
		chive	grave	oven	shave	vent	wave
		clover	gravy	over	shovel	vest	wavy

ve	/v/ ■pg95	above	curve	glove	loaves	receive	solve
		active	dove	halves	love	shove	starve
		calves	elves	leaves	move	sieve	swerve
		creative	give	live	olive	sleeve	wolves

| **v v** | /v/ ◆pg95 | divvy | revved | savvier | savvy | | |
| | | divvying | revving | savviest | skivvy | | |

w	/w/ ●pg97	swam	swim	twenty	walk	water	wood
		swan	swing	twin	wand	web	wooden
		sweat	swirl	waist	warm	wind	wool
		swede	towel	wait	wasp	wing	world
		sweet	twelve	waiter	watch	wink	worm

wh	/w/ ■pg97	anywhere	whale	where	whimper	whisk	whizz
		everywhere	what	whether	whines	whisker	whoa
		nowhere	wheat	which	whip	whisper	whoop
		somewhere	wheel	while	whiplash	whistle	whopper
		whack	when	whilst	whirl	white	why
	/h/ ◆pg43	who	whole	wholesale	wholly	whose	
		whoever	wholemeal	wholesome	whom	whosoever	

| **wo** | I /oo/ ■pg65 | two | twos | | | | |
| | | twofold | twosome | | | | |

wr	/r/ ■pg77	rewrite	wreath	wrestle	wrinkly	writer	wrongly
		unwrap	wreck	wriggly	wrist	writing	wrote
		wrap	wreckage	wrings	writ	written	wrought
		wrapper	wren	wrinkle	write	wrong	wrung

x	/k/+/s/ ●pg99	box	expert	extra	index	oxygen	sixty
		earwax	explore	fix	jinx	pixie	taxi
		exclude	extend	fox	max	relax	text
		excuse	extent	galaxy	mixer	six	wax
		exit	extinct	hexagon	next	sixteen	waxy
	/z/ ◆pg103	anxiety					
		xylophone					
	/g/+/z/ ◆pg103	exact	exam	example	exert	exile	existence
		exactly	examine	exempt	exhaust	exist	

xc	/k/+/s/ ◆pg99	exceed	excellent	excess	excite		
		excel	except	excessive	excited		

xe	/k/+/s/ ◆pg99	annexe	deluxe				
		axe	pickaxe				

y	/y/ ●pg101	barnyard	yank	yeast	yet	yoghurt	your
		farmyard	yard	yell	yike	yolk	yo-yo
		yacht	yarn	yellow	yippee	yolkless	yuck
		yam	yawn	yes	yoga	young	yum
	/ee/ ■pg35	bunny	crazy	happy	party	silly	tidy
		carry	fifty	jelly	pony	sorry	tiny
		city	funny	lorry	pretty	sunny	windy
	/igh/ ■pg47	by	fly	my	reply	sly	try
		cry	fry	myself	rhyme	spy	why
		deny	imply	outcry	shy	sty	
		dry	July	pry	sky	supply	
	/i/ ◆pg45	analyst	crystal	hymn	physical	symbol	typical
		analytic	cylinder	mystery	pygmy	symphony	
		catalyst	gym	physics	rhythm	system	

ye	/igh/ ◆pg47	bye					
		goodbye					

you	/ue/ ◆pg91	you	youthen				
		youth	youthful				

z	/z/ ●pg103	ablaze	freezer	hazel	maze	zebra	zip
		breezy	froze	horizon	prize	zed	zipper
		cozy	frozen	kazoo	size	zero	zone
		crazy	glazed	lizard	sneezed	zigzag	zoo
		dozen	graze	magazine	wizard	zillion	zoom
	/s/ ◆pg79	blitz	waltz				
		quartz					
	/zh/ ◆pg105	azure					
		seizure					

ze	/z/ ■pg103	breeze	freeze	froze	ooze	sneeze	squeeze
		bronze	frieze	maize	seize	snooze	wheeze

zz	/z/ ●pg103	abuzz	dizzy	frizz	guzzle	muzzle	quizzed
		blizzard	drizzle	frizzy	guzzler	nozzle	sizzle
		buzz	fizz	fuzz	jacuzzi	nuzzle	snazzy
		buzzer	fizzle	fuzzy	jazz	puzzle	swizzle
		dazzle	fizzy	grizzly	jazzy	puzzled	whizz

References

Cambridge Dictionary ~ https://dictionary.cambridge.org

Oxford English Dictionary ~ https://www.oed.com

IPA ~ https://www.internationalphoneticassociation.org/